Dedicated:

to God, author and source of all good things

to my wife, April

and in memory of Reverend Pauline Allen

green press
INITIATIVE

Happenstance Books is committed to preserving ancient forests and natural resources. We elected to print this title on 30% post consumer recycled paper, processed chlorine free. As a result, for this printing, we have saved:

33 Trees (40' tall and 6-8" diameter)
12,167 Gallons of Wastewater
23 million BTU's of Total Energy
1,562 Pounds of Solid Waste
2,931 Pounds of Greenhouse Gases

Happenstance Books made this paper choice because our printer, Thomson-Shore, Inc., is a member of Green Press Initiative, a nonprofit program dedicated to supporting authors, publishers, and suppliers in their efforts to reduce their use of fiber obtained from endangered forests.

For more information, visit www.greenpressinitiative.org

Environmental impact estimates were made using the Environmental Defense Paper Calculator. For more information visit: www.papercalculator.org.

Hero For Christ

Hero For Christ

30 Ways You Can Be More Like
Mother Teresa, Martin Luther King, Jr.,
& Twenty Other World Changing Christians

Christopher Sunami
illustrations by Michael Krone

Happenstance Press / KIT☉BA BOOKS
Columbus, Ohio

HERO FOR CHRIST
30 Ways You Can Be More Like Mother Teresa, Martin Luther King, Jr., and
Twenty Other World Changing Christians

Published by
Happenstance Press/Kitoba Books
413 Fairwood Avenue, Columbus, OH 43205
happenstance@kitoba.com, http://heroforchrist.com

Publisher's Cataloging-In-Publication Data
(Prepared by The Donohue Group, Inc.)

Sunami, Christopher.
Hero for Christ : 30 ways you can be more like Mother Teresa, Martin Luther
King, Jr., & twenty other world changing Christians / Christopher Sunami ;
illustrations by Michael Krone. -- 1st ed.
p. : ill. ; cm.
Includes bibliographical references and index.
ISBN: 978-0-9702438-2-9
1. Christians--Conduct of life. 2. Christian biography. I. Krone, Michael. II.
Title.
BV4501.3 .S86 2008
248.4/8   2007908992

Printed in the United States of America.

CONTENTS

PROFILES: 22 Heroes For Christ

INTRODUCTION

We live in a time that is hungry for heroes. Our world's need for extraordinary women and men is clear from the headlines in every newspaper: The advance of technology has multiplied our ability to destroy each other with weapons of war; we are facing an environmental crisis with the potential to threaten life as we know it; each day brings new clashes between people of different cultures and beliefs; and there are many places in the world where poverty and misery are getting worse, not better. In times such as these, we long for leaders with a hero's combination of extraordinary abilities and exemplary moral courage.

Unfortunately, such people are hard to find. The idols of popular culture offer little in the way of inspiration, and our era's self-proclaimed Christian leaders have proven as violent, greedy, intolerant and hypocritical as anyone from outside the church. It has reached the point where many who are loudly and visibly associated with Christianity seem disconnected from the teachings of Christ in both what they preach and what they practice. Yet we find inspiration when we focus less on those who misuse Christ's teachings, and more on the great figures of history who succeeded in living Jesus' message as fully as they could.

The figures profiled in this book all began life as ordinary people, emerging from humble backgrounds and unexceptional circumstances. They were not necessarily smarter, stronger, or more talented than those around them. Nor were they what we think of as "better" than other people.

Even the saints among them were not "saintlike" in the sense of being free from sin. They all had flaws, made mistakes, and gave in to temptations. Nearly all of them were criticized during their lives, and some continued to be criticized even after their deaths. Yet each one was transformed by an encounter with Jesus Christ, and a subsequent decision to live in accordance with Jesus' teachings. By their faith, rather than by their merits, they earned places among the great men and women of history. Some among them were revolutionaries, reformers, theologians or artists, who altered the fate of nations and the course of human thought and endeavor. Others were educators, ministers or entertainers, who touched people's lives and hearts on smaller scales, but in ways that were equally profound.

Those included in this book are drawn from all periods of history and from nations and cultures all around the world. Each one embodied through his or her actions one or more of thirty featured lessons in heroism drawn from the life and message of Jesus Christ. By embracing those teachings, they became the living representations of these Christian virtues and values. It is the author's hope that by following in their footsteps each one among us can learn to serve our troubled world as a new "Hero for Christ."

It is important to note, however, that no change in behaviors or record of accomplishments can take the place of the relationship with God through Christ. For that reason, this book is not primarily aimed at a general audience, but at an audience of committed Christians looking for ways to live more in accordance with their beliefs. Every chapter in this book seeks to build upon that foundation, and should be read with that goal kept firmly in mind.

GOSPEL LESSONS:
30 Ways to Be a Hero

NOTE: All Bible verses quoted in this book are from the Gospels (Matthew, Mark, Luke and John) and are original modernizations of the King James translation of the Bible (with occasional inspiration from other modern Bible translations). Readers are encouraged to check all quotes against their own favorite translation of the Bible.

① PUT GOD FIRST

He who loves his father or mother
more than me
is not worthy of me:
and he that loves his son or daughter
more than me
is not worthy of me.

Matthew 10:37

T wo of Jesus' closest disciples were sisters named Martha
and Mary. On one occasion, when Jesus came to visit their
household, the two sisters responded in very different ways.
Martha, who was hard-working and conscientious, went to a
lot of trouble and effort to make sure the house was in order.
Meanwhile, Mary did nothing but sit at Jesus' feet and listen
as he spoke. When Martha complained about her sister's
laziness, she was surprised to hear Jesus defend Mary's wise
decision. Mary had chosen to focus on what was necessary —
her relationship with God, through Jesus —rather than what
was merely "useful."

Another story told in the gospels concerns a rich young
man who strove to be a good person, who faithfully obeyed all
the Jewish commandments, and who felt compelled to follow
Jesus. When Jesus asked him to give up all that he owned,
however, he found himself unable to let go of his possessions.
As much as he loved God, he loved his belongings more.

Both stories have the same moral: If you want to be a
Hero for Christ, you have to put God first. Every Christian

Hero's journey begins with a personal relationship with God. This does not mean being always right, hearing a booming voice from the clouds, or gaining supernatural abilities. Instead it means placing your relationship with God above everything else in your life.

The true Christian Hero defines faith as an attitude towards life, and not just a set of beliefs. He or she combines complete trust in God with a complete willingness to accept God's will, no matter what that might mean. Real faith withholds nothing from God. Instead faith places everything in God's hands: hopes, dreams, possessions, beliefs, health, career, family members and even life itself.

Remember: (1) No one else can have your relationship with God for you. As good as it is to be around others who have a relationship with God, none of their relationships can be a substitute for your own. Even if your mother, father, sister, brother, husband, wife, pastor or priest has a relationship with God, you will still need to seek one for yourself. (2) No one should come between you and God. The relationship with God is the most important thing you own, and no one who has your best interests at heart will seek to take it away. (3) No one else is necessary for your personal relationship with God through Christ. Even your priest, pastor or minister can only be a guide for your journey

---

Every time you face a decision this week, try to make the choice you believe Jesus would want you to choose. If you aren't sure which choice is right, pray deeply, and then do what seems right to you.

STORIES ABOUT HEROES
PUTTING GOD FIRST

Mother Teresa: "Put God First"

"Put God First" is a lesson Mother Teresa lived from the time she was a little girl. Her mother, Drana, was a strongly religious woman who taught her children to trust in God in all circumstances. Drana's own faith was not shaken even after her husband, Nikola, was murdered because of his outspoken political beliefs. Instead she continued to teach Mother Teresa and her other children the importance of following God's will.

By the time she was eighteen, Mother Teresa had become convinced that God was calling her not only to become a nun, but also to serve as a missionary in India. Following what she had been taught by her mother, she accepted the mission even though it meant leaving her beloved family and homeland behind.

The decision was neither easy nor without challenges. Among these was the fact that Mother Teresa's brother Lazar was horrified that his sister wanted to "bury" herself (as he put it in a letter) in a convent. In addition, her commitment to India placed geographic barriers between her and her original home, and political changes soon made returning to her birthplace impossible. Although she did not know it at the time, her departure from home at age eighteen was the last time Mother Teresa would see her mother or sister alive.

Even so, she never doubted that she had made the right choice; and throughout life, she honored her mother's memory by being the servant of God Drana had encouraged her to become.

Total surrender consists in giving ourselves completely to God. Why must we give ourselves fully to God? Because God has given himself to us. If God, who owes nothing to us, is ready to impart to us no less than himself, shall we answer with just a fraction of ourselves? To give ourselves fully to God is a means of receiving God himself.

Mother Teresa, *Total Surrender*

Martin Luther King, Jr.: "Put God First"

The pathway towards putting God first was not a straightforward one for Martin Luther King, Jr. He grew up in a religious family, with a pastor for a father, yet childhood for him was a time of doubts and questions about the beliefs of the Christian faith. Even after becoming a minister as an adult, he still felt distanced and divided from God.

What changed King's life was encountering a situation beyond his control. It was the middle of January in the year 1956. King had recently become the head of an organization protesting segregation (the legalized separation of blacks and whites) on city buses in Montgomery, Alabama. It was King's first significant position of leadership, but it was more a role that had been thrust upon him than one he had chosen.

At the time, the protest was going poorly, and the city was putting up stiff resistance. Earlier in the month several people had been arrested, including King himself. In addition, there were increasingly believable threats of violence being made against the protestors and their families, a group that included not only King, but also his beloved wife Coretta, and their newborn infant daughter.

One night after midnight, King was awakened by a telephone call. An anonymous voice on the other end called him racial names and threatened his and his family's lives if they did not abandon the protest immediately. Too frightened to go back to sleep, King began to pace the floor and review his situation. He knew all too well that lynching, the use of public murder as a form of social control, was still a regular occurrence in the South. Furthermore, his recent experience in jail had made it clear that the police and local authorities were against him, and could not be looked to for protection.

His back was to the wall, and his first thought was to find some way of escaping from his position of leadership. It was then, however, at the moment of his deepest despair, that he finally reached out to the God he served but had never known. Letting go of his doubt, his preconceptions, and his need for control, he surrendered everything to God, and opened himself to guidance. When he did so, he heard, as recorded in his autobiography, the voice of Jesus speaking to him in words that were strong and clear: "Martin Luther, stand up for righteousness. Stand up for justice. Stand up for truth. And lo, I will be with you, even until the end of the world."

As Christians we must never surrender our supreme loyalty to any time-bound custom or earth-bound idea, for the heart of our universe is a higher reality —God and his kingdom of love —to which we must be conformed.
  Martin Luther King, Jr., "Transformed Nonconformist," Strength to Love

Mahalia Jackson: "Put God First"

Gospel pioneer Mahalia Jackson was baptized at age fifteen, over the objections of her stern aunt and guardian, who refused to believe her niece was old enough to realize the seriousness of her commitment. Nevertheless, Mahalia herself had no doubt that she was ready to commit her life to putting God first. Pleasing God remained her primary goal for the next forty-five years until her death at age sixty.

It was clear from early on that Jackson had been gifted with an extraordinary voice and sense of music. Throughout her life, however, there were many who tried to convince her she could achieve greater fame and success by giving up gospel music in favor of a secular sound. Among those were the executives at her record label, who wanted her to record blues songs, her close friend Louis Armstrong, who thought she should sing jazz, and even her own husband, Isaac Hockenhull, who tried to force her to sing opera.

Jackson enjoyed secular music, and had even taken musical inspiration from the great blues singer, Bessie Smith. When it came to her own music, however, she knew the foundation of her talent lay in the religious messages of her song choices, and in the resulting presence of God in her performances.

No one can hurt the gospel because the gospel is strong, like a two headed sword is strong… Sometimes you feel like you're so far from God, and then you know those deep songs have special meaning. They bring back the communication between yourself and God.

Mahalia Jackson, *Got to Tell It* (Schwerin)

Sundar Singh: "Put God First"

Sundar Singh was born into a family of Sikhs, an ethnic group that practices its own hereditary religion, and whose members take great pride in their traditions, beliefs and culture. From an early age, however, Singh was a religious seeker, who wanted to put God first, but who found himself unsatisfied by the religion of his ancestors.

At first Singh's father was encouraging and respectful when Singh decided to study other religions. When Singh decided to embrace Christianity, however, it was a different story. His father was horrified at the very idea. In his eyes it brought shame and disgrace to the whole family to have Singh proclaim Christ in defiance of their own ancestral religion. For the next year, he and the rest of the family used threats, bribes, and every other method at their disposal, in an attempt to get Singh to change his mind. They even went so far as to sue the local missionaries for having brainwashed their child, a case that collapsed only when Singh himself testified that it was his own reading of the Bible and not the missionaries that had brought about his conversion.

The final straw for Singh's family was when he cut off his hair, which is strictly forbidden in the Sikh religion. For a Sikh to cut his hair is considered a public renunciation of Sikhism. In a fit of rage and shame, Singh's father drove him out of the house and forbade him to ever return. A few hours later, as Singh traveled towards a community of missionaries, he was afflicted by a terrible stomachache. Upon arrival, he fell into a deep sickness that turned out to be caused by a poison that had been mixed into his last meal at home. His family, considering him already dead in spirit, had preferred that he die in actuality than that he live to bring them disgrace. That he survived was only due to prayer and medical attention. A close friend of his, who had been thrown out of his home at the same time and for the same reasons, turned out also to have been poisoned, and died during the night.

Despite the rejection of his own family and community, Singh's determination to persist as a disciple of Christ only increased, even though it meant trading the luxuries of his wealthy family's home for a life of poverty and bare subsistence. Years later, however, he received an unexpected joy when his estranged father contacted him with the news that he too had elected to become a Christian.

> *The thought then came to me, "Jesus Christ is not dead but living, it must be He Himself." So I fell at His feet and got this wonderful Peace which I could not get anywhere else. This is the joy I was wishing to get. This was heaven itself. When I got up, the vision had all disappeared; but although the vision disappeared the Peace and Joy have remained with me ever since.*
> Sundar Singh, *The Message of Sádhu Sundar Singh* (Streeter)

CLOSING PRAYER (*inspired by* John 6:38)

Dear Lord, all that I am and all that I have is a gift from you. I freely place all of myself back in your hands, to do with as you will. Amen.

② FIND YOUR OWN PATH

Didn't you know that my place is in my Father's house?

Luke 2:49

When Jesus was only twelve years old, his family went on a trip to Jerusalem. On the way home Mary and Joseph traveled for an entire day before they realized that Jesus was not with them. In panic, they spent an extra day retracing their steps back to Jerusalem, where they found the young Jesus sitting in a temple discussing the scriptures. When they questioned why he had stayed behind, Jesus answered that they should have known he would be found in the house of his Father, doing his Father's business. In saying this, he did not mean Joseph, the man who had adopted him, but rather God, his Father in Heaven.

Like Jesus, we must often follow our own pathways through life if we wish to attend to the business of our Heavenly Father. Due to the very nature of the world, and the societies in which we live, we are faced every day with messages and choices that run counter to the moral lessons of Christ. Often, these come when good people with good intentions ask us to participate in or endorse things we know are wrong. We must therefore learn to be firm in positioning ourselves against the destructive trends of modern life.

In addition, each of us is in this world as a unique individual, endowed by God with a personality and a sense of self that is not identical to that of anyone else. The individuality each of us possesses is a gift from God, and should be treated as such. Thus, a Christian Hero must not be afraid to disagree even with good people of obvious faith. When you have open-mindedly examined all sides of an issue, and tested your position through prayer and study, it becomes a moral responsibility to hold fast to your convictions, until such time as God guides you towards a change.

Make a list of the goals, dreams, values, beliefs, and personal traits that help define who you are as a person. Are you living in accordance with the things you wrote down?

STORIES ABOUT HEROES
FINDING THEIR OWN PATHS

Sundar Singh: "Find Your Own Path"

When Sundar Singh was twenty years old, he accepted an offer to study at St. John's Divinity College, an Anglican seminary in Lahore (now in Pakistan). Although he enjoyed the chance to study Christianity more deeply, he soon felt that the expectations of the seminary were coming between him and his vision of simple direct service to Christ and humanity. In particular it was expected that he would become officially and properly ordained, wear only standard European clerical robes, conduct worship exactly in accordance with the formal Anglican service, use only the Anglican hymnbook, and preach only at the times and in the places where he was directed by the church authorities.

Singh found these requirements intolerable. He had already decided that he could only be effective as an evangelist within India if he presented himself in a way that would make sense to other Indians. Accordingly, he had elected to wear exclusively the saffron-colored robe of a traditional Indian *sádhu* or wandering holy man. In addition, he was unwilling to surrender the freedom to go where Jesus called him, and to preach as the spirit moved him. He left seminary less than a year later, and never returned.

Once when I was traveling in Rajputana… there was a Brahman of high caste hurrying to the station. Overcome by the great heat, he fell down on the platform. The Anglo-Indian station-master was anxious to help him. He brought him some water in a white cup, but he would not take the water. He was so thirsty, but he said, "I cannot drink that water. I would prefer to die." "We are not asking you to eat this cup," they said to him. "I will not break my caste," he said, "I am willing to die." But when water was brought to him in his own brass vessel, he drank it eagerly. When it was brought to him in his own way he did not object. It is the same with the Water of Life. Indians do need the Water of Life, but not in the European cup.

Sundar Singh, *The Message of Sádhu Sundar Singh* (Streeter)

Mahalia Jackson: "Find Your Own Path"

One person who realized the value of finding her own path was gospel singer Mahalia Jackson. In addition to resisting those who suggested she sing kinds of music other than gospel, she also resisted those who wanted her to sing gospel in a different style than her own.

For example, when she first moved from New Orleans to Chicago she found that there were different expectations within the church for singers. At home, everyone had sung along with all the hymns, but in Chicago members of the congregation were expected to sit quietly and listen to the choir. Jackson found it impossible not to sing from the pews, but this country habit turned out to be to her advantage. Instead of condemnation, the sound of her powerful voice resonating from the back of the church garnered her first an invitation to join the choir, later a spot as a soloist and finally her first chance in the music business, as a part of the Johnson Gospel Singers, her church's touring band.

Even as a member of a recognized group, however, Jackson still encountered criticism from those who expected her sound to conform to that of everyone else. More than once she and the rest of the Johnson Gospel Singers were ordered to leave a church by a pastor who thought their music sounded too much like jazz and the blues.

Later in life, Jackson's friend and musical partner, Thomas Dorsey, who wrote many of the most celebrated gospel hymns of the time, tried to teach her how to breath in the right places and phrase the music properly. Once again, Jackson resisted, saying that she did not want to sound the same as every other stereotypical singer. In the end, even a superb musician like Dorsey had to acknowledge that she was making the choices that were right for her.

> *I just found myself doing what came natural to me.*
> Mahalia Jackson, *Got To Tell It* (Schwerin)

Mother Teresa: "Find Your Own Path"

In 1946, Mother Teresa had been a nun for fifteen years, most of which were spent as a teacher and as a principal in various Catholic girls' schools attached to the Convent of Loreto in Kolkata, India. In the fall of that year, however, she fell ill and was sent to Darjeeling to recover. While on the train, she had a mystical experience in which she heard the voice of Jesus calling her to find her own path in a new and different ministry.

Upon her return to Kolkata, Mother Teresa immediately applied to the local Archbishop for permission to leave the convent and minister directly to the poor of the city. Although the Archbishop respected her passion, he rejected her request. It was unheard of for a nun to live outside of a convent, and he was both afraid for her safety and skeptical about her chances of success.

Had it not been for her experience on the train, Mother Teresa's respect for the Archbishop and for the church hierarchy might have convinced her to abandon her vision. Instead, she persisted, knowing that her orders came from a higher authority. Eventually, the Archbishop agreed to forward her request to the Vatican in Rome. After an impatient year of waiting, Mother Teresa received a personal dispensation directly from the Pope, allowing her to live and work outside the convent "with God alone as her protector and guide."

> *Follow me out of the convent and into the streets. Be my hands and tend my sick. Be my feet and visit my lonely, my sick, my prisoners. Be my voice and calm the distressed, comfort the afflicted, help the dying to come home to me.*
>
> Mother Teresa, *Called To Love* (Raphael)

Martin Luther King, Jr.: "Find Your Own Path"

In 1963, Martin Luther King sat in a jail cell in Birmingham, Alabama, having once again been imprisoned for his protests against racial injustice. While there, he received an open letter from eight clergymen, including a rabbi and several local Catholic and Protestant bishops. In the letter, they condemned the protests, counseled patient waiting, and commended the police of Birmingham for their response to the situation.

Although the clergymen wanted him to join them in supporting the *status quo*, King had already found his own path, which was different from theirs. In reply to their letter, he composed a remarkable letter of his own, detailing both his commitment to his God-given mission, and his disappointment in the resistance he had encountered from other religious figures. Not only did that letter become a key document of the Civil Rights Movement, it also led to a change of heart for one of the signers of the original letter, Bishop Joseph Durick, who went on to become a strong advocate of civil rights.

The contemporary church is often a weak, ineffectual voice with an uncertain sound. It is so often the arch-supporter of the status quo. Far from being disturbed by the presence of the church, the power structure of the average community is consoled by the church's silent and often vocal sanction of things as they are.

But the judgment of God is upon the church as never before. If the church of today does not recapture the sacrificial spirit of the early church, it will lose its authentic ring, forfeit the loyalty of millions, and be dismissed as an irrelevant social club with no meaning for the twentieth century.

Martin Luther King, Jr., "Letter From a Birmingham Jail"

CLOSING PRAYER (*inspired by* Matthew 13:15-16)

Dear Lord, help me listen more to you than to the crowd. Amen.

③

STAND UP
FOR WHAT YOU BELIEVE

And you shall be brought before governors and kings
for my sake,
as a testimony against them and the Gentiles.
But when they deliver you up,
take no thought how or what you shall speak:
for what you shall speak shall be given you in that same hour.
For it is not you that speaks,
but the Spirit of your Father which speaks in you.

Matthew 10:18-20

When Jesus was arrested, he was taken before Pontius
Pilate, the local representative of the Roman government.
Pilate was a very powerful man, and he was puzzled by the
fact that Jesus was unafraid in his presence. "Don't you
know I have the power to decide whether you live or die?" he
asked. In complete confidence, Jesus answered that the
reason he was under Pilate's jurisdiction was because of the
will of God, and not for any reason to do with Pilate's earthly
authority.

Like Jesus, a Christian Hero speaks the truth according
to his or her understanding of God's will, regardless of who
might stand in opposition. Too often Christians are silent in
the face of injustice, because they fear or respect those who
are in authority. They buy into the myth that a real
Christian is never political. To be a true Christian Hero,

however, you must not avoid taking stances on social issues. Instead, you need to understand that every political choice involves a moral choice, and that every moral choice finds a foundation in your religious convictions.

Honoring your relationship with God involves making a commitment to human beings as God's children. This in turn means taking stands against the constant abuses of those children by society. The challenge for the Christian Hero is to take public moral stances without falling prey to the corruption and compromises of political gain.

This week, be an activist in a way that reflects your moral beliefs.

STORIES ABOUT HEROES
STANDING UP FOR WHAT THEY BELIEVE

Martin Luther King, Jr.:
"Stand Up For What You Believe"

The first significant conversation between Martin Luther King, Jr. and John F. Kennedy took place in 1961, not long after Kennedy's election. The two men had met once before, and Kennedy had helped secure King's release from jail several months earlier (when King had been imprisoned following a protest). If Kennedy had expected King to be meekly grateful, however, he was sadly mistaken.

Instead, like a modern prophet, King stood up for the vision he believed God had given him for the nation. He reminded the President in no uncertain terms of his promise to end discriminatory housing, and called upon him to sign a "Second Emancipation Proclamation" ending all segregation across the country. At the time, Kennedy thought King's goals were unrealistic and unreasonable. Ultimately, however, he came around to King's point of view, and in the summer of 1963, he proposed a wide-ranging Civil Rights bill aimed at bringing about the end to segregation King had proposed.

Following Kennedy's tragic assassination later that same year, it fell to his successor, Lyndon B. Johnson, to step forward and make the proposal into law. Even this, however, was not enough to satisfy King's moral vision. A brief year later he met with Johnson to demand immediate passage of a law protecting the rights of voters. Like Kennedy, Johnson initially thought King was unrealistic. He urged King to be patient, and wait for changes to take place gradually. It was only five months later, however, that the Voting Rights Act passed, with Johnson as its author and biggest supporter.

Then, in 1965, King gave a final moral challenge to the President, this time calling on him to end the war in Vietnam. It was long before the tide of public opinion turned against the disastrous conflict, and Johnson refused even to consider the idea. Although King would not live to see it, however, his stance proved once again to be prophetic when President Nixon called the war to a final end in 1973.

One may well ask, "How can you advocate breaking some laws and obeying others?" The answer is found in the fact that there are two types of laws: there are just and there are unjust laws. I would agree with St. Augustine that "An unjust law is no law at all."

Martin Luther King, Jr., "Letter From a Birmingham Jail"

Toyohiko Kagawa:
"Stand Up For What You Believe"

Throughout his life, the biggest criticisms faced by Japanese Christian leader Reverend Toyohiko Kagawa resulted from his uncompromising commitment to stand up for his belief in peace and non-violence. According to his reading of the Bible, every human life was sacred. The concept of killing for politics or national interests was anathema to him, a stance that made him unpopular in Japan's militaristic culture, particularly during the lead-up to World War II. When Japan and America entered into hostilities following the attack on Pearl Harbor, Kagawa's words of peace were seen as the mark of a traitor. All one hundred thirteen of his books were banned and immediately went out of print, and a court-order was issued forbidding him from making public speeches. Through it all, however, Kagawa remained steadfast in his commitment to peace. When the war finally ended, Kagawa regained his reputation as a national moral leader, and became a key figure in the reestablishment of peace under the terms of the American occupation.

Only through service to others can a man bring harmony and peace to the people.

Toyohiko Kagawa, *A Seed Shall Serve* (Simon)

Óscar Romero: "Stand Up For What You Believe"

Archbishop Óscar Romero of El Salvador stood up for what he believed by being a voice of God's truth to the world under circumstances that can only be described as extreme. Few places in the modern world have been more dangerous for professing Christians than El Salvador in the 1970's and 1980's.

The reasons behind this were rooted in the rule of El Salvador by fourteen wealthy families who controlled the government, the military and the lucrative coffee plantations. Over the course of years, they used their influence to force poor farmers off lands that they then absorbed into their plantations. Once the land was solely theirs, they were able to hire the workers back at starvation wages.

The church became involved in the conflict when priests and other clergymen began speaking out on behalf of the poor. As an educated, visible, vocal, and morally upright segment of the population, the dissident priests represented a threat to the government's control of the Salvadoran people. Accordingly, they were targeted for harassment, abuse and assassination.

The killings began with Father Rutilio Grande, a Jesuit priest and personal friend of Romero, who was shot to death on his way to Mass, together with two members of his parish. A distraught Romero called the president of El Salvador to demand an immediate police investigation of the murder. The president's refusal to respond was an eye-opening experience for Romero. It highlighted the corruption of the government, and the extent to which it was willing to sanction terrorist acts as a method of social control. In response, Romero cut off official relations with the government, boldly refusing to give their state-sponsored events and occasions the legitimacy of a religious endorsement.

Over the course of the next several years, five other priests, and numerous others connected to the Catholic Church were assassinated, all because of their support of the poor and the oppressed. In most cases, the killings were carried out by members of shadowy right-wing terrorist groups. The murders were never investigated, however, because the terrorists had the hidden support of the government, which benefited from the climate of fear they created. Nor did the chain of corruption stop at even the highest levels of the Salvadoran government. Instead, the government itself relied heavily on funding, support, and high-level military training from the United States. In the same way as the Salvadoran government was willing to ignore the crimes of the terrorists groups that served their interests, the United States was willing to turn a blind eye to the government's abuses of power because they served American financial and military interests in the region.

Instead of being intimidated by the brutal violence and powerful friends of those on the other side, however, Romero became more and more vocal in his criticisms of government corruption and the exploitation of the poor. He even went so far as to write an open letter appealing directly to Jimmy Carter, then president of the United States, asking for the immediate cessation of military aid to El Salvador.

On the eve of his death, Romero preached his last sermon directly to members of the military, as an appeal to end the killings of their brothers and sisters among the poor. The next day, he himself was shot to death at the altar of a chapel as he prepared to bless the wine and bread for Communion. He is remembered in El Salvador as a martyr for the liberation of the poor.

> We cannot segregate God's word
> from the historical reality in which it is proclaimed.
> It would not then be God's word.
> It would be history,
> it would be a pious book, a Bible that is just a book in our library.
> It becomes God's word
> because it vivifies,
> enlightens, contrasts,
> repudiates, praises,
> what is going on today in this society
>
> Óscar Romero, *The Violence of Love*

William Wilberforce:
"Stand Up For What You Believe"

The great British politician and abolitionist William Wilberforce spent his entire career speaking unpleasant truths to people who were opposed to hearing them. He did so because his faith convinced him to always stand up for what he believed, no matter who opposed him.

Wilberforce is most famous for having taken a position against slavery at a time when the slave trade was still central to the British economy. His willingness to oppose the crowd, however, also extended to other matters as well, most notably issues of war and peace. For example, he once gave a speech to Parliament advocating pacifism, right in the middle of a war between Britain and France. Beyond the public disapproval that inevitably followed, Wilberforce also had to face the anger of his best friend, a man he viewed as a brother, Prime Minister William Pitt. It was deeply distressing to Wilberforce to speak out against his oldest and closest companion, and he did so in the fear that he had ruined their friendship forever. Nevertheless, he felt a duty to God to obey the convictions of his conscience.

I need hardly say that the prospect of a public difference with Pitt is extremely painful to me, and though I trust this friendship for me sunk too deep in his heart to be soon worn out, I confess it hangs me like a weight I cannot remove… My spirits are hardly equal to the encounter. However, I hope it will please God to enable me to act the part of an honest man in this trying occasion.

William Wilberforce, *A Hero For Humanity* (Belmonte)

CLOSING PRAYER (*inspired by* Matthew 22:21)

Dear Lord, help me to free myself from those things that belong to those who rule and who oppress, so that I might better be able to give You all the things that are Yours. Amen.

PUT FAITH ABOVE "RELIGION"

Woe to you, religious scholars and Pharisees, hypocrites!
For you shut the doors of heaven against men.
You neither enter yourself,
nor let those who are entering go inside

Woe to you, religious scholars and Pharisees, hypocrites!
For you devour widow's houses,
then make a great show out of your long prayers;
therefore you shall receive the greater damnation

Woe to you, religious scholars and Pharisees, hypocrites!
For you cross both sea and land to make one convert,
and when he is converted,
you make him twice the child of hell as yourself

Matthew 23:13-15

The Bible shows that Jesus reserved his strongest words of condemnation neither for the prostitutes, adulterers, and corrupt officials who surrounded him; nor for Judas, his betrayer; nor even for Pilate, his executioner. Rather, his strictest sermons and harshest words were directed against those commonly considered the most righteous men of their times, a group of pious religious fundamentalists known as the Pharisees.

In the same way, it is the duty of the Christian Hero to speak out not only against the crimes and failings of the secular world, but also against those who misuse religion for their own ends. The fact that someone proclaims himself or herself a Christian does not mean that every word from his or her lips is gospel truth; nor should a self-proclaimed Christian be held to any less of a moral standard than anyone else. We live in a time where some of the loudest voices proclaiming their own Christianity are preaching messages of greed, intolerance, violence and self-righteousness, in direct opposition to the true teachings of Christ. No Christian Hero can remain silent while the Christian religion is abused by false prophets for profit and political gain. It is important for those who believe in Jesus' message of love to identify themselves as Christians, and for those who are Christians to advocate Jesus' message of love.

This week, take each religious message presented to you, and test it against the words of Christ.

STORIES ABOUT HEROES
PUTTING FAITH ABOVE "RELIGION"

Martin Luther: "Put Faith Above Religion"

Martin Luther, the German theologian who inspired the Protestant Reformation, is often thought of as an enemy of the Catholic Church.

In reality, he was an ordained Catholic monk who was devoted to the church, but horrified by corruption and abuses taking place within the church hierarchy. In particular, he felt called by God to put faith above religion by speaking out against a clergyman named Cardinal Albert of Mainz, who claimed to be able to sell divine forgiveness of sins for money.

By opposing Cardinal Albert, Luther not only took a stand against one corrupt clergyman, he also promoted the principle that a personal relationship with God was more important than a relationship with the church. By extension, this meant also that one's personal responsibilities to God outweighed responsibilities to any church official, from the humblest parish priest to the Pope himself.

Following the publication of his "Ninety-Five Theses" against church corruption, Luther made further strides in bringing ordinary individuals closer to God through his translation of the Bible into German. Previously, only Latin and Greek Bibles had been readily available, which meant that only highly educated people could read the Bible for themselves. Luther's work inspired translations of the Bible into many other languages, including English. In this way, he freed the message of Jesus from the prison of the church hierarchy. Although Martin Luther's bold stances eventually caused him to be excommunicated, he inspired important reforms both inside and outside the Catholic Church.

The church needs a reformation which is not the work of one man, namely, the pope, or of many men, namely the cardinals, both of which the most recent council has demonstrated, but it is the work of the whole world, indeed it is the work of God alone. However, only God who has created time knows the time for this reformation. In the meantime we cannot deny such manifest wrongs.

Martin Luther, "Explanations of the Ninety Five Theses"

Dorothy Day: "Put Faith Above Religion"

Dorothy Day's views often led her and the *Catholic Worker* newspaper she founded and edited to put faith above religion by taking stances counter to those adopted by many other Catholics, especially when it came to the issue of war. For example, during the Spanish Civil War, most Catholics initially supported General Franco, despite his fascist politics, because he was against Communism, and a supposed Catholic. Unlike some of her radical friends, Day did not feel comfortable endorsing the Spanish radicals, some of whom had shown a willingness to attack and persecute the Catholic Church. She neither felt comfortable, however, supporting a figure as repressive and brutal as Franco. Instead, she called for both sides to lay down their arms. This pacifist stance caused the paper to lose over two-thirds of its circulation, and virtually all its support from within the Catholic Church. Her position, however, was later vindicated by Franco's military support of Hitler and Mussolini during the Second World War.

> *…there were a very great many who had seemed to agree with us who did not realize for years that* The Catholic Worker *position implicated them; if they believed the things we wrote, they would be bound, sooner or later, to make decisions personally and to act upon them.*
>
> Dorothy Day, *The Long Loneliness*

Toyohiko Kagawa: "Put Faith Above Religion"

Christianity is a minority religion in Japan. Even so, religious leader Toyohiko Kagawa was always willing to put faith above religion by speaking out against those who were straying from Jesus' message, even if they were members of his own church. This was a habit he gained at age sixteen, when he became the youngest person enrolled at the Meiji Seminary. There, he became notorious among his classmates for his outspoken opposition to Japan's then-ongoing war against Russia. Even though the war was going badly, most people still considered it treason to make any criticism of Japan's government or foreign policy.

One night, Kagawa found a group of older seminary students waiting for him outside the dormitory. Sullen-faced and hostile, they questioned him on whether it was true that he thought Japan was making a mistake by continuing the war. Kagawa did not hesitate to answer. His reading of the gospels had convinced him that Jesus would support a path of peace. "Yes," he said boldly.

That was all the others needed to hear. Without another word, they began beating Kagawa with their fists. True to his belief in non-violence, however, he refused to fight back. A moment later, the ringleader of his tormentors signaled the others to stop. "What do you say now?" he said.

Bruised and bloodied, Kagawa made his way back to his feet. "Forgive them, Father," he quoted, "for they know not what they do."

> *It is most unfortunate that Protestants carry with them a sort of spirit of antagonism, and that the Roman Catholics take an attitude of intolerance.*
> Toyohiko Kagawa, *Christ and Japan*

Óscar Romero: "Put Faith Above Religion"

Archbishop Óscar Romero's calling to speak God's truth brought him not only into conflict with the Salvadoran government, but also with members of his own church. Once he had been like them, a believer that the church should maintain a good relationship with the government, and keep its own focus firmly on spiritual matters. As he became more aware of the injustices taking place around him, however, he became convinced that he could only be true to the teachings of Jesus through placing faith above religion, and aligning himself with the poor and the oppressed.

One of Romero's first and most controversial acts as Archbishop was what became known as the "Single Mass." It was held in memory of Father Rutilio Grande, who had been murdered because of his work on behalf of exploited farm and plantation laborers. Two Sundays after Grande's death, Romero issued a cancellation of all other Masses throughout his archdiocese. Every Catholic in El Salvador who wanted to celebrate Mass that week was forced to attend the commemoration of Father Rutilio's life and work. The hundred thousand who arrived on Sunday from around the country witnessed the previously mild-mannered and conservative Archbishop preaching a fiery sermon against the persecution of the church.

Among those outraged by Romero's unprecedented act was El Salvador's papal nuncio (ambassador from the Vatican), who called the Single Mass "irresponsible, imprudent and inconsistent." It was the start of three years of tension, not only between Romero and the nuncio, but also between Romero and many of El Salvador's other bishops, including some he had once counted as close friends. Before long, things had degenerated to the point where there were bishops openly attacking Romero in their reports to Rome, with some going so far as to accuse him of fomenting violence and supporting terrorism.

It was difficult for Romero to face opposition even within his own church, but his allegiance remained with God and God's poor. Accordingly he persisted in the path that he knew to be right, despite the accusations that he had sold out religion for politics. Eventually he was vindicated, both by the support given him by Pope John Paul II during his life, and by being declared a candidate for sainthood after his death.

> *A religion of Sunday Mass but of unjust weeks*
> *does not please the Lord.*
> *A religion of much praying but with hypocrisy in the heart*
> *is not Christian.*
> *A church that sets itself up only to be well off,*
> *to have a lot of money and comfort,*
> *but that forgets to protest injustices,*
> *would not be the true church of our divine Redeemer.*
>
> Óscar Romero, *The Violence of Love*

CLOSING PRAYER (*inspired by* First Kings 19:11-12)

Dear Lord, help me distinguish between your voice and all the noise that can surround it. Amen.

⑤
PRAY OFTEN

And all things that you shall ask in prayer, believing, you shall receive.

Matthew 21:22

A close reading of the gospels reveals Jesus praying on nearly every occasion. He prays alone after feeding the crowd of five thousand, again after healing Peter's mother-in-law, again after healing the man with leprosy, and yet again when healing the crazy man. He prays before naming and commissioning the Apostles. He prays on the mountain before the transfiguration. He prays at Gethsemane prior to facing his crucifixion, and he prays for his disciples on the occasion of the Last Supper.

Like Jesus, a Hero for Christ must seek constant communication with God through prayer. Every important occasion, every momentous choice, and every difficult task should be preceded by a prayer for help and guidance, and followed by a prayer of thanks.

This week, pray at least twice a day, once when getting up, and once when going to bed. In addition, pray before each important choice you make.

STORIES ABOUT HEROES IN PRAYER

Augustine: "Pray"

Saint Augustine is famous for having been a youthful sinner before he became a pillar of the church as an older man. In between, however, he went through several years of soul-searching and spiritual confusion. These years culminated in a crisis that Augustine experienced while sitting with a friend in his garden. He felt as though he were divided into two different selves, one of which wanted to follow God and one of which refused. Throwing himself down at the foot of a tree in the garden, Augustine wept and prayed. As he lay there, seeking God and an escape from his sins, he heard the voice of a child from a nearby house saying "take and read, take and read." Interpreting the child's words as a divine message, Augustine went to his Bible and read the first passage he encountered, advice from Saint Paul to give up fleshly pleasures. Reading the words gave Augustine the strength to win his internal battle, and he pledged himself in service to Jesus from that moment onward.

Cast yourself upon God and have no fear. He will not shrink away and let you fall. Cast yourself upon him without fear, for he will welcome you and cure you of your ills.

Augustine, *Confessions*

Sundar Singh: "Pray"

When Sádhu Sundar Singh was still young, he studied the teachings of many different religions. By the age of sixteen he had read the holy texts not only of his own ancestral religion of Sikhism, but also those of the Hindu and Islamic traditions as well. His strongest reaction, however, was to Christianity, a religion that he initially hated and despised. In his own words he was a "persecutor" of Christians, going so far as to publicly burn a Bible in front of his friends and family.

Despite his strong feelings, and his study of many religions, Singh felt a deep and unconquerable emptiness within his soul. In addition, he suffered from bouts of depression that had begun with the death of his beloved mother, a few years earlier. This combination of factors brought him to the brink of suicide, just a few days after his dramatic Bible-burning. Having awakened in the middle of the night, he was overcome by the urge to go out and throw himself in front of the five o'clock train. In the few hours left to him, however, he decided to make one last attempt at finding peace in life. Accordingly, he prayed that if any God or gods truly existed that he be shown the right pathway.

For over an hour and a half he prayed without receiving any answer, while all the time the fatal hour drew closer. Then, just before he was about to leave the house, Singh became conscious of a sensation of great light. To his shock, rather than an apparition of one of the Hindu gods and goddesses of his homeland, Singh perceived a vision of the same Jesus Christ whose religion he had so violently rejected. As he stared in amazement, he thought he heard a voice calling him in his own native language. When he accepted the invitation, he felt a profound sensation of the same peace and joy he had been longing for, but unable to find. As the vision faded from his eyes, he immediately went to wake his father, to tell him that he had become a servant of Jesus Christ.

Unsurprisingly, his father responded with disbelief. "Only three days ago you burned the Bible, and now you think you are a Christian? Leave me alone, and go back to sleep!"

> *If it had been some Hindu incarnation I would have prostrated myself before it. But it was the Lord Jesus Christ whom I had been insulting a few days before. I felt that a vision like this could not come out of my own imagination. I heard a voice saying in Hindustani, "How long will you persecute me? I have come to save you; you were praying to know the right way. Why do you not take it?"*
>
> Sundar Singh, *The Message of Sádhu Sundar Singh* (Streeter)

Toyohiko Kagawa: "Pray"

When Toyohiko Kagawa was a child he was introduced to Christianity by a local missionary. At the time, however, he was living in the home of his Buddhist uncle, who was very much opposed to Christianity. In an effort to hide his new faith from his uncle, Kagawa would go into his bedroom, put his covers over his head, and pray. For eight months, his only connection to Christianity was through his secret prayers. Despite not belonging to a church or communicating with other Christians during that time, he still felt himself growing in faith and becoming a better, stronger person, strictly through the power of his prayers. By the time the eight months were over, Kagawa was ready to live openly as a Christian, no matter what his uncle thought.

Later, when Kagawa was in college, he began preaching in the slums of Tokyo. On one occasion, he was preaching when a cold rain began to fall. Although he was very tired from his hard week, Kagawa was determined to finish his sermon. By the time he was done, he had lost his voice, and was running a fever. He spent the next two days in bed until someone finally sent for a doctor. When the doctor arrived, he diagnosed tubercular pneumonia and said there was no hope of a cure. By the time a week had passed, Kagawa could hardly breath, and the doctor said it was time to say goodbye to all his friends and loved ones.

As he lay there, waiting to die, Kagawa decided to pray. He prayed for the next four hours without a pause. At the end of the time, he began to feel a mysterious certainty that God was there with him, an "ecstatic consciousness" of God's love. Suddenly he coughed up a vast quantity of clotted blood. With the blood cleared from his lungs, he was able to breath again, and soon his fever had also broken. Although it would take Kagawa several more months to get well completely, it was the beginning of his recovery.

> *There is a lesson for us in the fact that Jesus prayed the whole night through. In long-continued meditation one draws nearer and nearer to God, until he makes his petitions not for the advancement of his own interests, but for the glory of God.*
>
> *Toyohiko Kagawa, Meditations on the Cross*

CLOSING PRAYER (*inspired by* Proverbs 3:5-8)

Dear Lord, help me remember always to seek your guidance. Amen.

⑥
BE HUMBLE

...for every one that exalts himself shall be humbled;
and he that humbles himself shall be exalted.

Luke 8:14

One of the stories Jesus told his disciples was about a pious
Pharisee who went to the temple at the same time as a tax
collector. In order to understand the story, we must
remember that the people of that time considered the
Pharisees to be the holiest of the holy people. They were
strict religious fundamentalists, and had a good reputation in
their communities. Tax collectors, on the other hand, were
more than just people who took away money from others.
They were employees of the hated Roman conquerors, so they
were considered traitors by their own people. In addition,
they all extorted extra money beyond what they gave to the
government, so they were considered to be liars and cheats as
well.

In the story, the man with the good reputation proudly
thanks God for his own righteousness. He carefully lists all
the sins he has avoided, and even mentions how glad he is to
be a better person than the tax collector praying beside him.
In contrast, the tax collector is weighed down by the
knowledge of his crimes. Not daring even to look
heavenward, he prays for mercy and forgiveness. Against
the expectations of the characters in the story, and probably
against the expectations of the audience as well, Jesus then

told his disciples that the sinful tax collector was the man who left the temple with God's blessing.

In the same way as the tax collector, the Christian Hero must be always humble and never proud. To be a Hero for Christ, you must remain more mindful of the harm of which you are capable of doing than of the good you believe you have already done. Furthermore, you must never be ashamed to seek God even when you are in the middle of wrongdoing for that is exactly the time when you need God the most. Only when you can confess your secret shames and misdeeds before God will you begin to heal and move forward.

This week, make a list of all the sins you have ever committed, all the sins you have ever contemplated, and all the sins you hope never to commit. Acknowledge yourself as a sinner, and ask God for forgiveness.

STORIES ABOUT HUMBLE HEROES

Sundar Singh: "Be Humble"

Having grown up in a society where holy men are often worshipped like deities, Sádhu Sundar Singh was always careful to make it clear that he was nothing more than a humble preacher of the Word of

Christ. He refused to accept any disciples, or to follow the urging of his supporters that he found an order of Christian *sádhus*. In his effort to deflect attention away from himself, he refused even to perform baptisms for those whom he inspired to accept Christianity, referring them instead to local churches or missions. He discouraged his biographers, and in all ways, he strove to be as unobtrusive as possible, so that Christ's work could be seen all the more clearly in his life, free from the distractions of his own persona.

> *Why should I be proud? ...When Christ rode an ass into Jerusalem, people brought clothes and laid them upon the road. Yet the feet of our Lord did not tread on them, only the ass walked over them. Who ever heard of such honour being done to the feet of an ass? It was only because the ass carried Christ. When He had done riding the ass, the beast was of no account. So I am of no account, only I am as it were bearing Christ, and it is Him you honour. If He left me I should be nothing at all.*
> Sundar Singh, *Called of God* (Parker)

Martin Luther: "Be Humble"

Although his influential writings made him the key figure in the Protestant Reformation, Martin Luther was humble enough to prefer that people pay more attention to his ideas than his person, and more attention to the Bible than to either. He always made it clear that his intentions had never been to gain personal notoriety, but only to bring people closer to God. Although he was a lifelong workaholic, who eventually wrote over one hundred thick volumes of theology, he often disparaged his own writing in favor of the Scriptures that had inspired him.

> I'd rather that all my books would disappear and the Holy Scriptures alone would be read. Otherwise we'll rely on such writings and let the Bible go. Brenz wrote such a big commentary on twelve chapters of Luke that it disgusts the reader to look into it. The same is true of my commentary on Galatians. I wonder who encourages this mania for writing! Who wants to buy such stout tomes? And if they're bought, who'll read them? And if they're read, who'll be edified by them?
>
> Martin Luther, *Table Talk*

Augustine: "Be Humble"

Saint Augustine of Hippo was born in North Africa in the year 354. His mother, Monica, was a devout Christian who always hoped her son would follow in her path. In his youth, however, this seemed like an unlikely possibility. Instead, the young Augustine pursued a life of hedonism and pleasure, taking a long-term mistress, and having a son out of wedlock. He also flirted with several other religions, being at first a Manichaean and then a pagan, before finally embracing Christianity on the cusp of middle age.

Augustine is far from being the only Christian to have a checkered past. Few others, however, have been humble enough to lay open their own personal weaknesses as did Augustine. His sins compose the most memorable portion of his master-work *Confessions*, sometimes described as the world's first autobiography. In it, Augustine details his sometimes-sordid past, with no attempt to make himself seem better or more noble than anyone else. He even includes his youthful prayer, "Lord, grant me celibacy... but not yet!"

Ironically, it is this honesty itself that has made *Confessions* one of the world's most widely read and influential Christian writings. Rather than driving people away with a pose of saintly perfection, Augustine invites even the most hardened, long-term or repeated sinner to share with him the joy of Christ's redeeming mercy and forgiveness. As a result, generations after generations of truth-seekers have experienced *Confessions* as a pathway to God through Christ.

> *I must now carry my thoughts back to the abominable things I did in those days, the sins of the flesh which defiled my soul. I do this, my God, not because I love those sins, but so that I may love you. For love of your love I shall retrace my wicked ways. The memory is bitter, but it will help me to savour your sweetness, the sweetness that does not deceive but brings real joy and never fails.*
>
> Augustine, *Confessions*

Thérèse of Lisieux: "Be Humble"

When Saint Thérèse of Lisieux was a child, she had a tendency to be impatient and willful. In particular she was unwilling to wait to reach adulthood in order to fulfill her lifelong dream of becoming a nun. Instead she went so far as to throw herself at the feet of the Pope himself to ask special permission to enter a convent at the early age of fifteen.

By the time she reached twenty-one, six years later, her eager girlhood wish for a life of religious glory had matured into a faith that was more calm, more patient, and more humble. In particular, she requested not to be promoted to the status of a full nun, despite having spent not only the required three years as a novice, but an additional three years prior to that as a postulant. This request was her way of shielding herself against the pride she knew she still possessed. By remaining a novice, she could hold on to the spiritual disciplines of novicehood, including the need to ask permission for even small decisions. As a perpetual novice she would also be excluded from positions of leadership and authority. In this way she could continue in the convent as a lifelong student.

> 'Remaining little' means--to recognise one's nothingness, to await everything from the Goodness of God, to avoid being too much troubled at our faults; finally, not to worry over amassing spiritual riches, not to be solicitous about anything.
>
> Thérèse of Lisieux, *The Little Flower of Jesus*

CLOSING PRAYER (*inspired by* Luke 18:13)

Dear Lord, have mercy on me, a sinner. Amen.

TAKE RESPONSIBILITY

And why do you see the speck in your brother's eye,
but never think about the plank in your own?
And how can you say to your brother
 "Let me pull the speck out of your eye"
when the plank is in your own?
You hypocrite, first cast the plank out of your own eye,
and then you will see clearly
to pluck the speck out of your brother's eye.

Matthew 7:3-5

One of Jesus' most famous sayings is that a man must take the plank out his own eye before searching for the speck in his brother's eye. Although this is well-taken as a warning against hypocrisy, it also holds an important secret about gaining more control over the world in which you live.

Too often, we look at our lives as being full of problems caused by others. We point fingers at criminals, bad people and evildoers, with the thought that getting rid of them would get rid of all evil in the world. This attitude, however, is what Jesus condemns as finding specks in the eyes of our brothers.

Instead, we should take each such evil we encounter, and ask ourselves if we are not supporting, enabling, or duplicating it in some way. Once we find our own contributions to the things we oppose, we gain power over them through the power to change our own behaviors. This is what Jesus calls taking the plank out of our own eyes.

Accordingly, a Hero for Christ must be willing to evaluate himself or herself as fully and as honestly as possible. To be a Christian Hero involves knowing yourself intimately, your weaknesses as well as your strengths. You cannot hide your failings from God, and you only endanger yourself and others when you hide them from yourself. Once you know and understand what you are doing wrong, however, you then gain the ability to start making it right.

Identify five bad or wrong things taking place in the world or in your life. For each one, identify some way, no matter how small, in which you are contributing to the problem, and then take steps to change your own behaviors.

A STORY ABOUT A HERO TAKING RESPONSIBILITY

Geoffrey Griffin: "Taking Responsibility"

Although largely unknown in the United States, the late Geoffrey Griffin was famed across Africa as one of the continent's premiere educators of school-aged children. His eventual destiny, however, would have been hard to predict from his initial choices. He was born in Kenya as the child of white British colonialists. He grew up as a loyal citizen of the British Empire and a supporter of the British rule of East Africa. Accordingly, when a rebellion against the British broke out in 1952, he made what he considered to be the patriotic choice, and joined the colonialist army.

As the conflict raged onwards, however, his opinions gradually began to shift. More and more, he began to respect the legitimacy of the native Kenyans' claims to the land of their ancestors. Although he was distressed by the violence and brutality of the rebel forces, he was increasingly aware that his own side was behaving in ways that were equally bad.

Eventually, Griffin came to understand that the best way to support his goals of peace and a bright future for Kenya were not to fight against an external enemy, but rather to make changes within himself. By taking personal responsibility for the violence tearing apart the land of his birth, he was able to make different and better choices. In this way, he eventually became an important part of the transition to Kenyan independence and self-rule.

> [I felt] more comfortable to be jobless than watching and giving people instructions to butcher and kill each other.
> Geoffrey Griffin, *Educating Modern Kenyans* (Otiato)

CLOSING PRAYER (*inspired by* Matthew 23:27-28)

Dear Lord, help me take responsibility for the world around me, and for my contribution to the evils of the world. Amen.

FORGIVE YOURSELF & MOVE FORWARD

When the unclean spirit has gone out of a man,
he walks through dry places, seeking rest, and finding none.
Then he says, "I will return into my house from where I came"
and when he returns, he finds it empty, swept, and tended.
Then he goes, and takes with him
seven other spirits more wicked than himself,
and they enter in and dwell there:
and the last state of that man is worse than the first.

Matthew 12:43-45

The Apostle Peter was one of the greatest Christian Heroes who ever lived, yet his record contained its fair share of flaws and failings. As the gospels tell it, Peter was at various times guilty of foolishness, weak faith, and even violence. By far his most serious misstep, however, was his triple denial of Christ. Just a few hours earlier, Peter had sworn to Jesus that he would never deny him. When Jesus was arrested, however, fear overtook Peter, and he swore in front of witnesses that he had never even met Jesus before.

Later, after the Resurrection, Jesus appeared to Peter. Taking him apart from the others, Jesus asked Peter the same question three times: "Peter, do you love me?" Each time that Peter answered yes, Jesus instructed him "Feed my sheep." With these three affirmations, Peter received a triple forgiveness for his triple denial. In return, he accepted his tripled responsibility to continue onwards in service to humanity as a disciple of Jesus.

The message is clear. Jesus is willing to forgive us of all our sins, no matter how severe; yet freedom from sin does not mean we are freed from our duty to do God's work on earth. Our forgiveness comes without price to us; yet it then becomes our responsibility to move forward with life. As Jesus said, he came so that we might have life "more abundantly." When we refuse to let go of our past and future faults, we abuse the forgiveness Jesus has granted us.

Another way of looking at it is that being a Christian frees us from the burden of perfection. We are all imperfect; we have all sinned and fallen short of the perfection of God. Accepting that fact, and knowing that God still loves us gives us strength to carry on, despite our failings.

On the other hand, as Jesus warns us, when our lives have nothing to fill the empty place where our sins used to be, we become vulnerable to committing new and worse crimes. But if we fill our lives with service to God and humanity, then our old sins will find no room in our lives to return. Thus, a Christian Hero must not only accept God's forgiveness, but also be willing to combine it with self-forgiveness. If you wish to be a Christian Hero, avoid wasting time on self-hatred and regrets. Instead, treat each new day as a new chance to move forward and do better.

This week, take your lists of sins and burn them. Then, write a new virtue, commitment or goal to replace every item on the old lists.

STORIES ABOUT HEROES
FORGIVING THEMSELVES

Martin Luther King, Jr.: "Forgive Yourself"

In January of 1964, Martin Luther King, Jr. was on the verge of beginning what would be one of his most important campaigns, in Selma, Alabama. His outspokenness had already won him many enemies, however, including J. Edgar Hoover, the harsh and devious head of the Federal Bureau of Investigations. It was Hoover who had a special package sent to King's wife Coretta. Inside was an audio tape giving evidence of an extramarital affair by King. Also included was a letter suggesting that King had one of three choices to make: to retire from the civil rights movement, to kill himself, or to face having his affairs publicly exposed.

It was a dark moment for King. He was fiercely devoted to his wife, and his infidelities were his greatest shame. In addition, he knew that public accusations of sexual misbehavior would damage his reputation as a moral leader. Nonetheless, he felt that his only real option was to do what he had always done, to forgive himself, to pray God for divine forgiveness, and to continue with the struggle.

In the end, although Hoover did in fact leak his surveillance tapes to the press, the media refused to participate in ruining King's reputation. Accordingly, King went ahead with the Selma campaign as planned. His subsequent victories there are often seen as the turning point in the Civil Rights Movement. They changed the opinions of many people around the nation, and paved the way for the passage of Lyndon B. Johnson's landmark Voting Rights Act.

> *Place your failure at the forefront of your mind and stare daringly at it. Ask yourself, "How may I transform this liability into an asset? How may I, confined in some narrow Roman cell and unable to reach life's Spain, transmute this dungeon of shame into a haven of redemptive suffering?"*
> Martin Luther King, "Shattered Dreams", *Strength to Love*

Geoffrey Griffin: "Forgive Yourself"

Although Kenyan educator Geoffrey Griffin began his career in a colonialist army, he soon reached the point where he could no longer in good conscience fight on the side of the British. Rather than chastise himself, however, for having fought for a cause he now believed to be unjust, he instead forgave himself, and turned his attention to what good he could do towards a better future for Kenya as a nation. Accordingly, and although the fighting still continued, he applied for a transfer to take over the administration of the juvenile segment of a detention facility.

The facility, known as Manyani, was a grim and abusive place that Griffin would later compare to the concentration camps of Nazi Germany. In addition to holding adult prisoners-of-war, Manyani also imprisoned minors under the age of sixteen who had been captured fighting for the rebels, as well as those whose parents were involved or suspected of involvement with the rebellion, and even ordinary delinquents, street children and orphans.

Under Griffin's leadership, Manyani slowly began to transform, a process that was accelerated when Griffin received permission to move all youth under the age of sixteen to a new facility. Over the next several years, this new location, called Wamamu, would slowly change from a high-security prison to a place that resembled a school. At the same time, Griffin, the former soldier and man of violence, was likewise transformed, into an educator and a man of peace.

> ...nothing could please me more than to be able to go forward. This was my country, I was born here, I love it, I've done some good things in it and I would love to do more.
>
> Geoffrey Griffin, *Educating Modern Kenyans* (Otiato)

CLOSING PRAYER (*inspired by* John 8:11)

Dear Lord, help me believe and accept the forgiveness you have given me, so that I might move forward in life as an instrument of your love, Amen.

⑨

DEVELOP YOUR TALENTS

He who received five talents came
and brought five other talents,
saying "Lord, you gave me five talents:
Behold, I have gained five additional ones as well."
His lord said to him,
"Well done, you good and faithful servant:
you have been faithful over a few things,
I will make you ruler over many.
Enter into the joy of your lord."

Matthew 25:20-21

Jesus tells a story of a lord who entrusted each of his servants with a large sum of money before leaving on a trip. While he was away the servant he entrusted with the largest sum of money doubled it through wise investments. The same was true of the servant to whom he gave the next largest sum of money. But the servant he trusted with the least amount of money did nothing but bury it in the ground.

When the lord returned, he praised the first two servants for the good work they had done with their opportunity. But he scolded the third servant, took back what he had given him, and gave it instead to the servant who had the most. In telling this parable, Jesus warns us we are expected to make full use of every talent, skill and opportunity we receive in life. This is an especially crucial lesson for those of us who live in societies with material wealth, social opportunity, and civil liberties. There is no excuse for us not to do incredible things with the resources we have.

If you want to be a Hero for Christ, a good start is to develop your talents to their fullest extent, and put them to work in the service of God and humanity. By doing this, you progress towards becoming your ideal self. At the same time you pay homage to the work of God the creator, who made you the unique, irreplaceable individual that you are.

Write a list with two columns. In the first column, write all your undeveloped aptitudes –things you think you could do well if you only tried. In the second column, write every skill you do not have but wish you did. Pick one aptitude to develop, and one skill to gain, and spend time over the next month developing them into talents.

STORIES ABOUT HEROES DEVELOPING THEIR TALENTS

C. S. Lewis: "Develop Your Talents"

Author C.S. Lewis was a great believer in the idea that all good things come from God. Accordingly, he was willing to develop all his talents and to give them free play –because he was convinced that everything of value he created with them would have its source in

God, and thus be in service to God. This confidence sometimes led him in directions that were unusual or unique.

For example, although he wrote many works of conventional theology, Lewis is perhaps better known for his works of science fiction and fantasy. Both are genres which are often considered as antithetical to religion: science fiction, because the scientific worldview is considered to have a bias towards atheistic rationalism, and fantasy, because it is founded heavily in mythology and the occult, and thus considered to have a bias towards false religions and superstitions.

Lewis, however, accepted neither of these arguments. He strongly maintained that belief in God and Christianity was not only completely rational, but more rational than atheism, and thus compatible with a scientific worldview. At the same time, he also believed that the mystic occurrences of fantasy were echoes, reflections, and preparations for what he called the "One True Myth," the narrative of the Bible, which combined the miraculous nature of the events imagined in fantasy and mythology with the actualized reality of divine intervention in the world.

Because of this, Lewis felt comfortable allowing his deep Christian faith to influence his writing, even in the "forbidden" genres. In doing so, he was ignoring the advice of his close friend, J.R.R. Tolkien, who, although also a committed Christian and a fantasy writer, chose to keep his two worlds as separate as possible. Lewis, however, had reason to believe that the path he was choosing could bear good fruit, since his own conversion to Christianity had been influenced by the work of the Scottish fantasy author (and ordained minister) George MacDonald.

In the end, the enduring reputation of Lewis is based as strongly on the popularity of his children's fantasy series, *The Chronicles of Narnia* as it is on his works of theology. Although many have read these books strictly as entertainment, they are also an avenue for Lewis to consider some of the weightiest issues of Christian faith. In this way, they have been a significant religious influence on more than one generation of young readers.

> Now the story of Christ is simply a true myth: a myth working on us in the same way as the others, but with this tremendous difference that it really happened: and one must be content to accept it in the same way, remembering that it is God's myth where the other are men's myths.
>
> C.S. Lewis, *A Biography* (Green)

Martin Luther King, Jr.: "Develop Your Talents"

From the time he was young, Martin Luther King, Jr. had a gift with words. Even as a child, his passion for reading and incredible vocabulary astounded those around him. Once, when a teacher asked him what he was doing, he playfully responded: "Cogitating with the cosmic universe, I surmise that my physical equilibrium is organically quiescent."

As he matured, however, King began to see a value to his gift that went beyond his youthful pleasure in the pure sounds and meanings of words. When he was a teenager he had been scornful of the raw passion of the traditional black church experience. As an adult, however, King learned to combine the emotional religious faith of his father's generation of preachers with the elaborated arguments for social change of figures such as Gandhi, Thoreau, R. Niebuhr and Rauschenbusch.

It was this potent mixture of bedrock faith, emotional appeal, intellectual argument, social vision and Biblical language that made King into the greatest orator of modern times. He had developed a talent for expression that transformed the moral commitments of an entire generation.

> *At the beginning of the protest, the people called on me to serve as their spokesman. In accepting this responsibility, my mind, consciously or unconsciously, was driven back to the Sermon on the Mount and the Gandhian method of nonviolent resistance. This principle became the guiding light of our movement. Christ furnished the spirit and the motivation and Gandhi furnished the method.*
>   Martin Luther King, Jr., "Pilgrimage to Nonviolence", *Strength to Love*

Michelangelo: "Develop Your Talents"

One of the greatest artists of all time was Michelangelo Buonarroti, who was born in 1475 at the height of the Italian Renaissance. Like other artists of his era, he produced work on many themes (including some drawn from Greek and Roman mythology), yet it is his work on Christian subjects that represents the fullest fruition of his artistry. Even today, five hundred years after his death, he is famous around the world for his monumental work on the ceiling of the Sistene Chapel. There, he portrayed Biblical scenes with such confidence and power that his portraits of the *Creation of Adam* and the *Expulsion From the Garden of Eden* remain the dominant images of those events in the popular imagination. Equally as well-known as these is another Michelangelo work on a Biblical theme, the *David*, which (appropriately enough) is a portrait of a great artist of the Biblical era.

A devout and regular churchgoer, and a deeply spiritual man, Michelangelo always referred to his talents as "given by God." Late in life, he even went so far as to deny that any human artist had ever taught him or inspired his work. Rather, he insisted that he was directly inspired to develop his talents by the craftsmanship of the greatest artist in the universe, God, the Creator.

The prayers I make will then be sweet indeed,
If Thou the spirit give by which I pray:
My unassisted heart is barren clay,
Which of its native self can nothing feed:
Of good and pious works Thou art the seed,
Which quickens only where Thou say'st it may;
Unless Thou show to us Thine own true way,
No man can find it: Father! Thou must lead.
Do Thou, then, breathe those thoughts into my mind
By which such virtue may in me be bred
That in Thy holy footsteps I may tread;
The fetters of my tongue do Thou unbind,
That I may have the power to sing of Thee,
And sound Thy praises everlastingly.

Michelangelo, translated by William Wordsworth

CLOSING PRAYER (*inspired by* Matthew 25:20-21)

Dear Lord, help me make the best possible use of the talents you have given me. Amen.

LIVE YOUR FAITH

Beware of false prophets, who come to you in sheep's clothing, but inwardly they are ravenous wolves. You shall know them by their fruits. Do men gather grapes of thorns, or figs of thistles? Even so, every good tree brings forth good fruit, but a corrupt tree brings forth evil fruit. A good tree cannot bring forth evil fruit, neither can a corrupt tree bring forth good fruit. Every tree that does not bring forth good fruit is cut down and cast into the fire. Therefore by their fruits you shall know them.

Matthew 7:15-20

One morning, Jesus and his disciples passed a fig tree growing by the side of the road. Jesus searched the tree for figs, but did not find any, which was unsurprising, as it was not the right season. Seemingly in anger, he was heard to say that no one would ever eat figs from that tree again.

Later the same day, Jesus and the disciples arrived at a temple. Those who were there were not praying, but instead carrying on all manner of business: buying and selling and exchanging money. Again in seeming anger, Jesus overturned the tables of the salesmen and drove them out of the temple.

That evening, Jesus and the disciples passed the same fig tree they had encountered in the morning. In those few short hours, it had withered away. When the disciples called attention to the tree, Jesus told them it was all a matter of faith.

Although the disciples may have not realized it, the fig tree was a living metaphor for the events of the day. One of the teachings of Jesus repeated most often throughout the gospels is that a good tree bears good fruit —meaning that good people take good actions, and thus produce good results. The temple, however, was like an unfruitful tree, or a tree with bad fruit. The people there were not good people, and although they pretended to be religious, they were really concerned only with making money.

The punishment of the money-changers and the death of the tree were both warnings to the disciples: that life is short, and that none of us knows how much time we have to "bear good fruit." Whether or not figs were in season, the tree should have brought forth fruit for Jesus. The fact that it could not do so was an indication of its spiritual deadness.

There has long been an argument among Christians about which is more important, faith, or good works. This is a false choice. If your faith is true, you will be inspired to be a better person and do better things. If, on the other hand, there are no good deeds to your credit, it is a sign that you are not living your faith. A true Hero for Christ should strive to put faith in action every hour of every day.

Take one skill or talent you have already, and find a new way to put it to use in the service of God and humanity. Be creative. For example, if your talent is singing, one obvious choice would be to join your church's choir. A more unusual way to please God, however, might be to put on a free concert for people in a homeless shelter, hospital or nursing home.

STORIES ABOUT HEROES LIVING THEIR FAITH

William Wilberforce: "Live Your Faith"

British abolitionist William Wilberforce considered the true embrace of faith to be the one that manifested in the actions of the believer. His own return to Christianity had not come in a sudden religious epiphany. Rather, he became gradually convinced of the truths of Christianity at the same time as he began to live out his faith by applying Christian moral principles in his life. The stronger that faith became, the less willing he was to go along with the cheap tricks and petty corruption of politics; and the more committed he became to larger moral causes such as the end of slavery and the promotion of peace.

In this, Wilberforce was following the example of his spiritual mentor, John Newton, who is best remembered as the composer of the hymn *Amazing Grace*. Newton had been a Christian from his youth onwards, even as he undertook the morally reprehensible profession of slave trader. As the years passed, however, the progression of his faith gradually shifted his views to the point where he viewed slavery as an abomination against humanity and a sin in the eyes of God. Accordingly, he became one of the earliest and most influential voices against Britain's slave trade.

Although Newton had been a believer in Christ for most of his life, it was only in old age that he considered himself to be living the life of a true Christian. It was a process that Wilberforce called "the Great Change." If it truly took root in a person's life, the effects would spread until his or her character, views, and actions had all been transformed for the better.

> I am anxious to see decisive marks of your having begun to undergo the great change. I come again and again to look to see if it really be begun, just as a gardener walks up again and again to examine his fruit trees and see if his peaches are set; if they are swelling and becoming larger, finally if they are becoming ripe and rosy.
>
> William Wilberforce (in a letter to his son, Samuel)
> *A Hero For Humanity* (Belmonte)

Toyohiko Kagawa: "Live Your Faith"

Japanese Christian leader Reverend Toyohiko Kagawa believed that a person cannot preach the gospel without also living his or her faith as fully as possible. Accordingly, from the start of his career, he turned all his available resources solely to the purpose of serving others. For example, while still a seminary student, Kagawa took the money allotted to him for his own living expenses and used it to feed and shelter the poor.

Later in life, he took his considerable gifts as a writer and put them to similar use. His numerous novels, works of theology, philosophy and economics all served multiple functions. At a direct level, they were meant to serve as a source of comfort or inspiration for those who read them. At a second level, they were meant to promote social change and reform within Japan. At a third level, however, they were a source of income that Kagawa unfailingly used on behalf of those less fortunate than himself.

> The more we are blessed, the more we owe the world. The higher the waterfall, the greater the amount of energy it should create. If water stays on the mountain top or above the dam, it creates no energy. We cannot create new social energy by staying aloof, with no thought of the world about us. We must be active in the affairs of the world.
>
> Toyohiko Kagawa, *A Seed Shall Serve* (Simon)

Mahalia Jackson: "Live Your Faith"

No one disputes the fact that Mahalia Jackson had ample talent, and the natural power of her voice was a great asset to her career in the days before electric amplification became common. In a world filled with talented people, however, what made her distinctive was the way she brought her faith to life. Part of what people responded to when they heard Jackson sing was how her love for God and humanity came through in her voice. It was clear that she was never just singing words on a page, like so many other singers. Rather, each word came from her heart. Moreover, there was a warm and a genuine quality to her performances that could neither be duplicated nor disguised.

Beyond the qualities she brought to her performances, however, was the way that Jackson used her talent to further larger causes in which she believed. Having grown up in the segregated American South, Jackson was always conscious of her position as an ambassador for black America. By touching the lives of people of all nations and colors through her music, she hoped to also change their hearts and opinions with regards to race.

In addition, Jackson took things a step further through her personal support of the Civil Rights Movement. She was most famously involved through her performance of *I Been 'Buked and I Been Scorned,* just prior to the introduction of Martin Luther King, Jr. at the 1963 March on Washington. She had entered the movement years earlier, however, in a quieter but more dangerous way, when she performed a benefit concert in Montgomery Alabama to help fund the boycott of segregated public buses. It was only a short time later that the home she had stayed in was bombed, completely destroying the room in which she had stayed. Even so, Jackson never doubted she had made the right choice.

I been 'buked and I been scorned
I'm gonna tell my Lord
When I get home
Just how long you been treating me wrong.
            (The words of one of Mahalia Jackson's favorite spirituals)

CLOSING PRAYER (*inspired by* Matthew 12:35)
Dear Lord, help me live my faith as an instrument of your love; and bless my efforts that they might bear good fruit. Amen.

SERVE THE LEAST

Then the King shall say to those on his right hand,
"Come, you blessed of my Father,
inherit the kingdom prepared for you
from the foundation of the world:
For I was hungry and you gave me food;
thirsty, and you gave me a drink;
I was a stranger and you took me in;
naked and you clothed me;
sick and you visited me;
I was in prison and you came to visit me.

Then the righteous will answer, saying
"Lord, when did we see you hungry and fed you?
Or thirsty and gave you a drink?
When did we see you a stranger and took you in?
Or naked and clothed you?
And when did we see you sick, or in prison, and visited you?

And the King will answer, and say
"Truly, I tell you,
what you have done for one of the least of these my brothers,
you have done for me."

Matthew 25:34-40

According to the prophesy of the "Last Judgment," everyone
will be gathered in front of Jesus on the last day of time, and
judged according to one simple criteria. It will not be
whether you are a sinner, whether you went to church, what

beliefs you professed, or what your sexual habits were. Rather, the blessed will be those who have ministered to the needs of "the least" of their brothers and sisters. They will be those who fed the hungry, gave water to the thirsty, clothed the naked, welcomed strangers, ministered to the sick and visited those who were imprisoned.

Conversely, the cursed will be those who failed to feed the hungry, failed to give water to the thirsty, did not clothe the naked, did not welcome strangers, did not minister to the sick and did not visit those who were imprisoned. According to this prophesy, therefore, the sole determinant of whether Jesus will be pleased or displeased with your life is how you treat those in need around you.

This means that every community of Christian Heroes must be dedicated to serving the "least": the poorest, the hungriest, the weakest, the youngest, the least advantaged, the most vulnerable and the most oppressed human beings. As Jesus said, there are no blessings for those who seek good things only for themselves, or for people who love only those who love them back. Instead, a blessed community serves even those who can offer nothing in return.

Do research on the area in which you live. Who qualifies as the "least" in your area? Who are the most poor, oppressed, needy or vulnerable people whose lives touch your own? Identify five things you can do to help them with their immediate needs. Additionally, identify five ways you can reach out to them socially (rather than just with charity).

STORIES ABOUT HEROES SERVING THE LEAST

Mother Teresa: "Serve the Least"

The reason Mother Teresa is known all over the world is because of the fullness of her commitment to live out Jesus' call to serve the least, and to see each human being as an embodiment of Christ. From the moment she left her convent, she worked tirelessly on behalf of those who were among the poorest of all the poor on the planet. In her years in Kolkata she worked with the homeless, those without food, those without water, those missing arms and legs, those sick and those dying.

In a story told by one of her biographers, Mother Teresa once discovered one of her novice nuns attending to a man in the care of the order. Because the man's open wounds stank and oozed pus, the nun tried to clean them from a distance. Taking the man's care into her own hands, Mother Teresa scolded the nun, telling her to realize that in taking care of the man, she was taking care of Jesus himself.

> *You have to realize that this is Jesus. We are cleansing His wounds. We could not do this work if we did not believe it was the body of Christ we are taking care of.*
>
> Mother Teresa, *Called to Love* (Raphael)

Martin Luther King, Jr.: "Serve the Least"

Even after his successes fighting segregation in the South, Martin Luther King, Jr. refused to rest on his laurels. Instead, he turned his attention to a population that was one of the poorest and most dispossessed in the nation, the ghetto-dwellers of Chicago. In doing so he was determined to not only serve the least, but also to live among them, and experience life as did they. Accordingly, he moved his entire family, including his own young children, into a slum called Lawndale, a place he described as an "island of poverty" in an "ocean of plenty." There, he and his family were surrounded by horrors such as the attack by rats of a baby in a nearby apartment. Moreover, and to his distress, he noted that even his own children suffered negative changes in their personalities within a few days of their arrival. Nevertheless, the family stayed firm for nearly a year, using their own physical presence among the least as a way to call attention to the savage inequities of ghetto life.

The slum of Lawndale was truly an island of poverty in the midst of an ocean of plenty. Chicago boasted the highest per capita income of any city in the world, but you would never believe it looking out of the windows of my apartment in the slum of Lawndale. From this vantage point you saw only hundreds of children playing in the streets.
Martin Luther King, Jr. *The Autobiography of Martin Luther King, Jr.*

Geoffrey Griffin: "Serve the Least"

"Starehe Boys Centre and School" is an institution known internationally for academic excellence. When Kenyan educator Geoffrey Griffin first started it, however, he did not seek out children of the rich and the powerful, or even children with good academic records and test scores. Instead, he started his school as a service to the "least" among his own community, the homeless, orphaned and destitute street children of Nairobi.

Starehe was started in two ragged tin huts, which served as homes for seventeen former street children. It was presented to the public as a community recreation center in order to escape the bureaucratic regulations and administrative burdens placed on schools. Meanwhile, the program's underpaid staff worked overtime to give their often-difficult charges a complete academic, moral, spiritual and practical education.

Over the years what had originally begun as a refuge of last resort began to gain a reputation, first as the equal, and then as the superior of many of the more conventional schools around it. A place that once drew only students with nowhere else to go is now overwhelmed with eager applicants.

Even so, Starehe continues to honor its original mission of service to the least. A third of the students are charged at rates proportional to their family's income, while the remaining two-thirds of the places at the school continue to be reserved exclusively for students who are destitute.

> *Loitering on the streets of Nairobi were many helpless children especially boys left as orphans due to the deaths of their fathers during the Mau Mau struggles or as a result of the imprisonment of their fathers in detention camps. These kids wore tattered clothes, walked barefoot, and had nowhere to sleep, leave alone where to bathe. They had no food to eat and indeed looked very dirty, helpless and sickly. Their future was dark. For their daily survival they ate left-overs thrown into the dustbins and the older ones had to pickpocket in order to find money to buy food. They slept by the riverbanks, in shrubs, and in some city corridors in the cold, thus being exposed to all manner of dangers including diseases.*
>
> Hongo & Mugambi, *Starehe Boys Centre*

Toyohiko Kagawa: "Serve the Least"

When Reverend Toyohiko Kagawa of Japan was still enrolled in seminary, he decided that living in a comfortable dormitory was no way to learn to be Christlike. Instead, despite his poor health and unfinished classes, he decided to move off-campus and into a nearby slum. There he knew he would receive his true religious education, by serving the least among the wretched of his nation.

The house he chose to rent was not only tiny and rundown, it also had a reputation in the neighborhood for being haunted. Despite this, it was no more than a few weeks before the homeless in the neighborhood appeared at Kagawa's door, begging for shelter. Soon he had several roommates drawn from among the outcasts of society, including a murderer who had just been released from prison, a local beggar, and a man whose illnesses gave him open and oozing sores. The four of them lived together, crammed into two tiny rooms, and surviving on the meager ten dollars a month that Kagawa was able to save from his scholarship and his part-time job. Once the money had been divided among the four of them it was only enough to buy two meals a day, and that often nothing more than plain rice and water.

As Kagawa persisted in his newfound poverty, his classmates and professors at seminary, who initially thought he was crazy, began to admire and respect the depth of his commitment to Christ's mission. They took up collections to help support him, but instead of spending the money on himself, he rented a larger place for the sole purpose of taking in more of the neighborhood's destitute. Soon he was also playing host to an elderly couple too old and too sick to work, a delinquent orphan boy, a paralyzed beggar woman, and eventually five others, for a total of thirteen people. For a brief period of time he was even named as the foster father of a newborn infant whose mother was being sent to prison; and all this while continuing his studies for the ministry.

God dwells among the lowliest of men. He sits on the dust heap among the prison convicts. He is with the juvenile delinquents. He stands at the door begging bread. He throngs with beggars at the place of alms. He is among the sick, and with the unemployed in front of the free employment bureau.
Toyohiko Kagawa, *A Seed Shall Serve* (Simon)

CLOSING PRAYER (*inspired by* Matthew 25:40)
Dear Lord, help me see you in the least among the people I encounter each day. Help me see you in the homeless man who asks for spare change on the corner. Help me see you in the welfare mother standing in line at the grocery store. Help me see you in the special-needs child at school. Help me see you in the refugee or illegal alien who comes to this country without knowing the language or the culture. Help me see you in all those whom the world sees as worthless. Amen.

BE INCLUSIVE

When Jesus heard it, he was astonished, and said to those that followed, "Truly I tell you, I have not found faith this great within the nation of Israel. And I tell you that many shall come from the east and west, and shall sit down with Abraham, and Isaac, and Jacob in the kingdom of heaven."

Matthew 8:10-11

The Gospel of John tells us that Jesus once traveled through the country of a people called the Samaritans. Although the Samaritans and the Israelites were closely related, they hated and despised each other, with the Israelites considering themselves many times better than their poorer, less-educated, less-cultured cousins the Samaritans. Nonetheless, while he was in Samaria, Jesus stopped and asked a Samaritan woman for a drink of water.

At first the woman was shocked that any Jew would condescend to speak to her. As they continued to talk, however, she was wise enough to perceive that Jesus was sent by God. Accordingly, she took the opportunity to ask for the answer to an important question: Was it correct to worship God on top of the mountains, as the Samaritans did, or were the Israelites correct to claim that God must solely be worshiped within the temples in Jerusalem? In other words, which side was right, the Samaritans or the Jews?

Instead of picking sides, Jesus told her that God would soon be worshipped neither on the mountain nor in the temple, but in "Spirit and in Truth." By extension, this meant that God was not merely God of the Jews or God of the Samaritans, but rather God of all who were willing and able to worship him in the way that Jesus described.

A community of Christian Heroes must be an inclusive community. The more successful you are at bringing together people of different ages, races, cultures and backgrounds, the more blessings your community will receive. When we are inclusive, we follow the example of Jesus. He embraced Samaritans, who were despised and discriminated against, and Romans, who were the hated foreign oppressors. He called people of "all nations" to come sit at his table.

In order to be blessed, we must do the same. If the early Christians had not overcome their own racial and cultural prejudices, the vast majority of Christians in the world would never have had the chance to hear Jesus' message.

Identify ten ways to welcome people who are different from you into your community. Make sure you invite them into full membership and into leadership roles, rather than forcing them to "fit in" with how things have always been done.

STORIES ABOUT HEROES BEING INCLUSIVE

Geoffrey Griffin: "Be Inclusive"

Kenyan educator Geoffrey Griffin had a commitment to inclusion in every facet of his school, Starehe. Although he viewed religion as a key part of his students' education (and although he himself was a Christian) he never thought it was his place to dictate to his students what faith they should follow. Instead, he guided each student towards establishing or deepening a relationship with God, under the guidance of whatever faith that student professed when entering the school. Accordingly, each student was required to attend religious services, but exclusively within their own faith. As a living symbol of the brotherhood he hoped would one day exist throughout the world, Griffin erected both a Christian chapel and an Islamic mosque on Starehe's grounds. This inclusive spirit became a crucial factor in Griffin's ability to serve students from all parts of Kenya (which has a majority Christian population, but which is also home to a sizable minority of devout Muslims).

As controversial and as rare as the religious brotherhood practiced at Starehe is the brotherhood there between the rich and the poor. Starehe began as a refuge for destitute, homeless and delinquent boys. As its academic reputation began to grow, however, there was an increasing demand that it also be opened to students from less impoverished homes. To the surprise of many, Griffin agreed.

Against complaints that he had forgotten the school's original mission, or endangered its status as a charity, he explained that he did not want his students to be isolated by socioeconomic class. In other words, he did not feel that his students' poverty meant they should only be able to interact with other poor students. He thought it would be good for boys from rich and poor homes to live together, play together, eat and sleep together and attend classes together.

> *… over and above the emphasis on self-discipline, voluntary service and high academic achievement, the boys are encouraged to develop and excel, along their chosen path, in their personal faith in Almighty God. Whatever faith a boy professes on entry, Starehe will do its best to help him advance and strengthen himself within it.*
>
> Geoffrey Griffin, *School Mastery*

Martin Luther King, Jr.: "Be Inclusive"

The life work of Martin Luther King, Jr. was to live out the message of Christ's all-inclusive love. Over and over he stressed the need of America to come together as a united nation, undivided by race, class, religion and ethnicity.

King's commitment to inclusion was no less in relationship to his life and organizations. He counted Mahatma Gandhi, the great Indian leader, as a personal hero, despite the fact that Gandhi was a Hindu. Furthermore, his closest advisors included Stanley Levison, who was

Jewish, and Bayard Rustin, who was both homosexual and a gay-rights advocate.

Ironically, King's commitment to live out his principles in his own life caused him to come under attack by other members of the Civil Rights Movement. Black leaders such as Stokely Carmichael (later "Kwame Ture") and Malcolm X (later "El-Hajj Malik El-Shabazz") rejected the call for an integrated America, instead advocating black separatism, as well as all-black political groups, communities and nations.

What these others failed to grasp, however, was that the principle of inclusion had a practical side as well as a moral side. King knew that white Americans would only favor justice for black Americans if they saw America as a unified whole, rather than as two battling sub-nations. It was necessary for them to identify with their black brothers and sisters, so that an injury to any given person would be felt as an injury to all, regardless of the race of the victim.

For example, it was only after white civil rights activists were murdered by segregationists that American public opinion shifted decisively against segregation. Those white volunteers who would have been excluded by the black separatists instead became crucial martyrs to the cause.

Another thing that disturbs me about the American church is that you have a white church and a Negro church. How can segregation exist in the true Body of Christ? I am told that there is more integration within the entertaining world and other secular agencies than there is in the Christian church. How appalling this is!
        Martin Luther King, Jr., "Paul's Letter to American Christians"
                                              Strength to Love

Mother Teresa: "Be Inclusive"

Mother Teresa was as devout a Catholic as could be imagined, and always hoped and sought to bring people into the community of God's love through Christ. She never, however, refused anyone care on the basis of their religious beliefs, or on the basis of any other characteristic such as race or ethnicity. She was even inclusive enough to allow those dying in her care to be attended by those of their own religion, and in accordance with the last rites of their own faiths, whether those might be Muslim, Hindu, Buddhist, Protestant, Catholic or Jewish.

For example, Mother Teresa once took in a dying Hindu priest from a rival religious organization in the same neighborhood. As the man died, she herself brought him water from the Ganges River, which is considered sacred within the Hindu religion. Even though the man was neither a Christian, nor a friend to Christianity, Mother Teresa still saw within him Christ, who comes in the form of those around us who need our help. In the end, by refusing to exclude nonbelievers, Mother Teresa's Missionaries of Charity brought hundreds of thousands more people to Christ than might have a similar organization that ministered only to Christians.

In 1969, Mother Teresa took another important step toward inclusion when she founded the "International Association of Co-Workers of Mother Teresa." This was a group made up of people of all faiths, not just Catholics or other Christians. They supported the Missionaries through prayers and service, and became the first ever multi-faith organization to be officially connected with a Roman Catholic order.

Even late in her life, Mother Teresa's commitment to inclusion remained strong. In 1985, she opened New York City's first hospice shelter for those dying of AIDS. Just a few months earlier, the Roman Catholic Archdiocese of New York had abandoned a similar plan for an AIDS facility after experiencing a wave of opposition from its parishioners. At the time, AIDS was seen as a disease of homosexuals and drug users, and there were many who refused to minister to those they saw as reaping the just wages of sin. Mother Teresa, on the other hand, had no patience for such prejudice. Her hospice opened on Christmas Eve of that year, just a few short months after the idea had first been proposed.

> We will not attempt to convert people of other faiths to Christianity or other Christians to Catholicism. We will see every human being as Christ, and we will help Hindus to be better Hindus, Muslims to be better Muslims, and Christians to be better Christians, by helping them to come closer to God.
> Mother Teresa, *Called to Love* (Raphael)

CLOSING PRAYER (*Inspired by* Matthew 28:18-20)

Dear Lord, as different as we are, help us come together as your loyal servants. Amen.

VALUE EACH INDIVIDUAL

Two sparrows can be bought for a dime, yet not one of them falls to the ground without your Father. But even the hairs on your head are numbered. So do not be afraid, you are worth more than many sparrows.

Matthew 10:29-31

One of Jesus' parables tells the story of a shepherd who has a flock of one hundred sheep. When he discovers a single sheep is missing from his flock, he leaves the others and goes searching high and low throughout the wilderness until he finds his lost sheep. Moreover, once he has found the sheep, he is filled with more joy for having found the one that was lost than in having kept the ninety-nine that never went astray. In the same way, God cares about each of us individually, and assigns our lives infinite value. There is more rejoicing in heaven over a single human being who turns to God than over all the angels that never went astray.

If God views our lives as infinitely valuable, then we must do the same. Accordingly, a Hero for Christ must value each and every individual. As Jesus told us, God views every single human life as important. God knows and loves each of us as individuals, and never gives up on any among us. We and our communities must do the same.

Find a person who belongs to a group, race, profession or class of people you have always disliked, dismissed or ignored. Find a way to see and to value that person as an individual, and as a beloved child of God.

STORIES ABOUT HEROES VALUING EACH INDIVIDUAL

Mother Teresa: "Value Each Individual"

Mother Teresa believed strongly that every single human life was valuable in the eyes of God, and thus that it needed to be in our eyes as well. Her chief goal in starting each of her many programs worldwide was to ensure that no person should ever have to live or die unloved and alone.

As an example, she once found an old woman abandoned on the street by her son, attacked by insects, and dying of illness and hunger. When the local hospital refused to admit the woman, Mother Teresa decided on the spot to open a hospice home for the sick and dying, so that even in a city of millions no one should have to die with neither dignity nor loving care.

Again and again, compassion for a single individual, or for a tiny group of people in need, was the impetus for one of Mother Teresa's large works. On another occasion, Mother Teresa was walking down the street when she came face to face with the horrifying sight of an abandoned newborn baby being dragged down the street by a stray dog. Although she rescued the child, it died soon afterwards. It was this event that led Mother Teresa to open her first children's home, a place where unwanted children and infants could be brought so that they could be cared for with love rather than neglect. On yet another occasion, Mother Teresa encountered five lepers who had been abandoned by families that were afraid to catch their illness. Less than a year later, she had opened her first "mobile clinic" for lepers, a traveling van that ministered to those with the disease.

Her ability to see people as individuals also extended to those whom most others saw merely as symbols or icons. For example, her friendship with Princess Diana was much reported in the media, which presented it as a relationship founded on the mutual fame of two "celebrities." For Mother Teresa, however, Diana was not a princess, but simply a fellow child of God, neither more nor less infinitely valuable than the poorest beggar on the Kolkata streets.

In the same way, Mother Teresa prayed often over the years that her biographer, Malcolm Muggeridge, would come to know the joy of a personal relationship with Christ. This was not a reflection of the fact that he had chronicled her life and work, or even of the fact that his television interviews with her had brought global attention and support to her programs. Rather, it was simply a reflection of the fact that he was a fellow human being, and that each individual human life was important to her.

By each action done to [the sick and the dying] I quench the thirst of Jesus for love of that person –by giving God's love in me to that particular person. How often we do not do that well!

Mother Teresa, *Total Surrender*

Toyohiko Kagawa: "Value Each Individual"

When Reverend Toyohiko Kagawa was a young child, he knew what it was to be ignored and unloved. His father died when he was young, and his mother, who was his father's mistress, died soon afterward. The orphaned Kagawa was left to be taken in by his father's wife, who surely saw him as an uncomfortable reminder of her late husband's infidelity. Later, he was shuttled between the homes of other relatives, including his older brother, a wasteful playboy who spent his time in gambling and womanizing, and his uncle, a strict and joyless Buddhist. Each viewed him more as an imposition than as a blessing.

It is perhaps for this reason that Kagawa responded so strongly when he encountered a Christian missionary who told him that God in heaven loved him personally. Not only did the missionary preach a message of love, but he also seemed to care about Kagawa as an individual. It was perhaps this, more than anything else, that made Kagawa wish to become a Christian.

Later, the same missionary served again as a role model during a time when Kagawa was quarantined for being gravely and contagiously ill. Even when Kagawa's own family stayed away, the missionary came and slept in the same room, despite the high risk of contagion.

It was this caliber of personal love that Kagawa endeavored to show others from that point onwards. He became a lifelong friend to the unwanted and unloved children of the slums, and like his hero the missionary, he was unafraid to sleep side-by-side with the sick and the contagious. Despite having grown up within a culture that devalued individuality, he was a tireless advocate of treating each and every human being as a creature of infinite worth.

> *In the heart of the God of the universe, each child of his is as necessary to him as are the fingers are to the hand. In the marvelous design of the universe, not even a sparrow can fall to the earth meaninglessly.*
> Toyohiko Kagawa, *Meditations on the Cross*

Sundar Singh: "Value Each Individual"

Sádhu Sundar Singh traveled often to Tibet, where he frequently preached Christianity to those who had never heard of it before. On one such occasion, he traveled across a treacherous mountain range, together with another man who did not wish to cross alone. In the middle of their journey, they were caught in a terrible snowstorm, with the result that the temperature plunged to almost unlivable levels.

As the two of them struggled towards the remote village that was their destination, they passed a body lying below. It was a man who had apparently fallen from the trail and been knocked unconscious. Singh immediately suggested that they go help the man, but his traveling companion refused, calling him a fool, and saying that the fallen traveler must be dead or as good as dead already, and that they would surely lose their own lives if they tried to help. Accordingly, he went on ahead and alone, while Singh made his way down the precarious slope, and somehow managed to carry the fallen traveler back up. He later credited the warmth he gained from his efforts in rescuing the unconscious man with raising his body temperature to the point where he was able to survive the remaining distance to the village. His other companion, however, never made it, and was later found frozen to death in the snow, presumably after having stopped to rest. Singh had been saved by his commitment to value each individual, while his companion's self-saving outlook had instead led to his doom.

> *If a piece of cold iron is placed in a hot fire it will glow because the fire is in it. Yet we cannot say that the iron is fire or the fire is iron. So in Jesus Christ we retain our identity; He in us and we in Him, but with our own individuality.*
> Sundar Singh, *Called of God* (Parker)

CLOSING PRAYER (*inspired by* Matthew 18:10)

Dear Lord, help me treat every human life as a valuable gift from you, Amen.

FORGIVE THE SINS
AND DEBTS OF OTHERS

Therefore, be merciful, as your Father also is merciful. Judge not and you will not be judged; do not condemn and you shall not be condemned; forgive, and you shall be forgiven. Give and it shall be given unto you; good measure, pressed down, and shaken together, and running over, shall men place in your lap. For the same measurement that measures what you give will measure what you receive.

Luke 6:36-38

One day Jesus was confronted by a group of respected religious men who had captured a woman in the act of adultery. According to the Law of Moses, the community was commanded to stone the woman to death in the middle of the public square. Accordingly, the men challenged Jesus with a no-win choice: either to join them in killing the woman, or to break the religious laws.

Instead, Jesus spoke the famous words, "Let he who is without sin cast the first stone."

One by one each of the accusing mob crept shamefaced away, each one knowing in his heart that he too was guilty of sins for which he had not been punished. When the last of the accusers had left the square, Jesus asked the woman "Has no one condemned you?"

"No, Lord," she answered.

"Then neither do I condemn you," said Jesus. "Go forth and sin no more."

Too many Christians consider it their primary job to loudly condemn the sins of the world. Yet a true Christian Hero heeds Jesus' warning: "Do not judge others, or you will also be judged." Our job as Christians is to bring others to Christ, and to serve as good examples by our own behaviors. Everything else is up to God. Whether others do well or badly is not our business. A blessed community passes judgment on no one, not even those —be they criminals, murderers, racists, prostitutes, terrorists or sexual offenders - whom the world judges most harshly.

Identify those in your community you have passed judgment on, either publicly, or in the quietness of your heart. Be like Jesus, and love them instead of condemning them. If you have condemned them quietly, then forgive them quietly. But if you have condemned them publicly, then forgive them publicly, and ask their forgiveness in turn.

STORIES ABOUT HEROES FORGIVING OTHERS

Mother Teresa: "Forgive Others"

Over the years, Mother Teresa came in for her fair share of criticism, much of which centered on her refusal to judge those with whom she associated. She was known for accepting funds with no questions asked, even if the donors had known criminal connections, or worked for corporations engaged in murky and immoral business practices. She also maintained friendships with dictators such as the Duvaliers of Haiti, and was sometimes accused of burnishing the image of more than one irredeemable figure at the cost of cheapening her own reputation.

What is lost in this picture is the fact that Mother Teresa did not reserve judgment only with regards to the wealthy, the famous, or the powerful. Rather, her habit was to not criticize anyone. Although she was vocal in opposition to practices she disagreed with, such as war and abortion, she was careful to separate her criticism of such practices from criticism of the person or persons involved. She knew that she herself (as well as even the most devoted of her missionaries or volunteers) was a flawed human being who fell short of the Glory of God. Given this, how could she avoid forgiving others, even those whose crimes seemed monstrous or manifest?

> If you judge people, you have no time to love them.
>
> Mother Teresa

Martin Luther King, Jr.: "Forgive Others"

For Martin Luther King, Jr., forgiving others was not only a personal commitment; it was a centerpiece of his non-violent approach to social change. Like Mother Teresa, he was careful to separate between acts he found morally reprehensible and those persons engaged in such acts. Thus, even though he fought against segregation, he never saw his enemy as the segregationists themselves, but only as the system they represented. His goal was never for the other side to be destroyed, but rather for them to experience redemption and reconciliation.

A third characteristic of this method is that the attack is directed against forces of evil rather than against persons who happen to be doing the evil. It is evil that the nonviolent resister seeks to defeat, not the person victimized by evil. If he is opposing racial injustice, the nonviolent resister has the vision to see that the basic tension is not between races. As I like to say to the people in Montgomery: The tension in this city is not between white people and Negro people. The tension is, at bottom, between justice and injustice, between the forces of light and the forces of darkness. And if there is a victory, it will be a victory not merely for fifty thousand Negroes, but a victory for justice and the forces of light. We are out to defeat injustice and not white persons who may be unjust.

Martin Luther King, Jr., *"Six Principles of Nonviolence"*

Toyohiko Kagawa: "Forgive Others"

Reverend Toyohiko Kagawa had a steadfast commitment to forgive others for their past actions. He went so far as to share his own home with men and women who had been convicted of crimes as severe as murder. He took the concept even a step beyond this, however, by giving attention to the literal meaning of Christ's words "forgive us our debts, as we forgive our debtors," where the word "debt" refers to financial obligations as well as moral ones. In this interpretation,

Christ calls on us not only to refrain from judging one another morally, but also to forgive any financial obligations owed to us by others.

Accordingly, Kagawa did not believe that true Christian love could coexist with economic exploitation. Because of this, he was a strong critic not only of the violence, atheism and fatalism of Communism, but also of the selfishness, loan-sharking and materialism of Capitalism. He believed that the only path forward for Christians was to seek an economic system founded on Christ's message of generous love.

> *Christ put God first, but in so doing, He did not ignore economics. He taught us that if we would store up treasure in heaven, we must share our treasure with the poor here, and give to those who ask, and not deny the borrower. We should do unto others as we would that they should do to us, and thus make our economic life God-centered.*
>
> Toyohiko Kagawa, *Brotherhood Economics*

CLOSING PRAYER (*inspired by* Luke 12:14)

Dear Lord, help me relate to others without judging or condemning them, Amen.

(15)

HONOR SERVICE

Among the unbelievers, those who rule flaunt their control over their people, and those who are considered great are those who wield authority. But it shall not be so for you. Whoever would be great among you would be one who ministers to the others, and whoever would be the chief of all must be the servant of all. For the Son of Man came not to be ministered unto, but to minister, and to give his life as a ransom for many.

Mark 10:42-45

One day, as Jesus and his disciples were traveling to Capernaum, the disciples began to quarrel about which one of them should be considered the greatest. In response, Jesus told them "If any man desires to be first, that same man should be the last of all and the servant of all." On another occasion, two of Jesus' disciples, James and John, the sons of Zebedee, came to ask Jesus that they might be allowed to sit on his right and left in heaven. This made the other disciples angry, but Jesus simply repeated what he had told them before: That anyone who wished to be great should become a servant, and that the person who was the greatest of all would be the person who served all others.

To the disciples, it must have seemed like Jesus was giving them a stern rebuke for their competitive, status-seeking ways. A closer look at Jesus' words, however, reveals a quite different message. Far from discouraging competition, Jesus is actually urging his disciples to outdo one another. They are not, however, being encouraged to struggle for wealth, power, possessions and authority; and neither are they in a race towards the "best seats in heaven." Instead, the greatest Christian is defined as the one who best serves others. In the secular world, money and power are what bring respect, but a Christian Hero honors those who serve best, and not those who have the most possessions. This is because Christ, our leader, was the servant of all humanity.

Beyond striving to be a good servant himself or herself, however, a Christian Hero must also honor service in others, and live in a community that gives service the highest honors. A Christian community can become strong and happy only when it takes respect and honor away from the rich and the powerful, and gives it instead to those who are the best servants, with the highest status reserved for those who do the most humble services.

Identify ten ways to give honor and respect to those in your community who provide the most service to others. Make sure you consider all different kinds of service.

STORIES ABOUT HEROES HONORING SERVICE

Martin Luther King, Jr.: "Honor Service"

And so Jesus gave us a new norm of greatness. If you want to be important—wonderful. If you want to be recognized—wonderful. If you want to be great—wonderful. But recognize that he who is greatest among you shall be your servant. That's a new definition of greatness.

And this morning, the thing that I like about it: by giving that definition of greatness, it means that everybody can be great, because everybody can serve. You don't have to have a college degree to serve. You don't have to make your subject and your verb agree to serve. You don't have to know about Plato and Aristotle to serve. You don't have to know Einstein's theory of relativity to serve. You don't have to know the second theory of thermodynamics in physics to serve. You only need a heart full of grace, a soul generated by love. And you can be that servant.

Martin Luther King, Jr "The Drum Major Instinct," *I Have A Dream*

Geoffrey Griffin: "Honor Service"

Kenyan educator Geoffrey Griffin honored service as an essential part of the Starehe Boys Centre curriculum. While all the boys participate in providing service to the school itself, a number of them go above and beyond the school's requirements by participating in what is called the "Voluntary Service Scheme." The students themselves started the program early in the school's history. Since the overwhelming majority of them were completely destitute, they felt an urge to do something to show their gratitude for the generosity they had received when they were admitted to the school. Accordingly, they arranged to take their own vacation time and spend it volunteering in community service projects. Although the first year only included seven students, the program had grown to over one hundred participants only two years later. By the time the program was ten years old, over half of the students were involved. According to the rules of the program, each needed to devote at least three of their vacation weeks to the program, none could accept any money or other compensation, and all had to be willing to accept any task, no matter how difficult, menial or tedious, and perform it cheerfully and to the best of their ability.

Despite the challenging requirements of the Voluntary Service Scheme, it continues to be one of Starehe's most popular and successful programs, providing untold numbers of service hours to hospitals, clinics and health centers, rural schools and libraries, public works projects, factories, airlines, broadcasting stations, bus companies and government offices.

My dear boys, I have enjoyed a fruitful and happy life, and I learnt one great lesson that I would like to share with you. I hope that Starehe will always teach this lesson –for as long as it does so, it will remain a great school. Our world is full of people who do their duty half-heartedly, grudgingly and poorly. Don't be like them. Whatever is your duty; complete it as fully and perfectly as you possibly can. And when you have finished your own duty, go on to spare some of your own time and talent in service to less fortunate people, not for any reward whatsoever, but simply because it is the right thing to do. Follow my advice in this and I assure you that your lives will be both happy and successful.

Geoffrey Griffin, *Educating Modern Kenyans* (Otiato)

CLOSING PRAYER (*inspired by* Luke 22:25-26)

Dear Lord, help me honor service more than wealth, and generosity more than power, Amen.

16

MENTOR OTHERS

You call me Master and Lord, and you speak well, for so I am. If I, then, your Lord and Master, have washed your feet, you ought to also wash one another's feet. For I have given you an example, that you should do as I have done. Truly, truly I tell you, the servant is not greater than his lord, neither is the messenger greater than he who sends him. It is good to know these things, but a blessing to do them.

John 13:13-17

After the Last Supper, one of the last things Jesus did with his disciples before his arrest was to wash their feet. The disciples found this very surprising, and Peter went so far as forbid Jesus to perform such a menial task for him. Jesus, however, warned Peter that if he did not allow Jesus to serve him in this way, then he would have no part in the Christian community. "In that case," announced Peter, with his typical enthusiasm, "then bathe the rest of me!"

Although Peter did not understand it at the time, the footwashing was symbolic. Through that act, Jesus was giving his disciples a complete blueprint for Christian Mentorship: a key practice that places a society of Christian Heroes under different rules and values than the secular world.

Acting in accordance with six principles, Service, Leadership, Respect, Education, Hierarchy and Action, the Christian Mentor is a servant who leads through his or her service. He or she is a teacher as well as a person of action, whose reputation is founded more on the successes of his or her students than on personal accomplishments.

The inspiration for these principles can be found in the things that Jesus said and did on the occasion mentioned above:

1. The washing of feet reminds us that a Christian Hero must be in **service** to others. The fact that it is the washing of the humblest part of the body represents an ethic that no service is too humble, too menial or too personal to be embraced.

2. The warning that Jesus gives Peter reminds us that it is through service to his or her followers that the Christian **leader** brings people into his or her community. Someone who refuses the service of the leader has "no part" in the community.

3. Jesus next reminds his disciples that he is still their Lord and Master. This inspires us to give our servant leaders their full measure of honor and **respect**, despite the humbleness of their service.

4. Jesus next explains that he is giving the disciples an example to follow. This inspires us to include a **teaching** aspect to our mentorship. The Christian Hero must be a teacher as well as a servant and a leader. He or she teaches both how to serve and how to lead.

5. Jesus then offers a reminder that the servant is not greater than the master, or the messenger greater than the one who sends the messenger. This reminds us that there is still a **hierarchy** in the mentorship relationship. The mentor outranks those whom he or she mentors, and their successes add to the reputation

of their mentor more than it adds to their own, just as our successes in our lives as Christians must be credited to Jesus rather than ourselves. Thus, the reputation of the student can never surpass that of the teacher, nor can the reputation of the mentored surpass that of the mentor.

6. Jesus finishes with the statement that it is more blessed to do these things then to know them —a pointed reminder that he expects his disciples to put what they have learned into **action**.

A mentor is a combination of a teacher and friend. A good mentor does everything possible to help those being mentored to succeed. He or she teaches them things they need to know, encourages them, provides them with resources, offers them feedback and in every other way works on their behalf. As Jesus said, the greatest blessings come to those who not only do right themselves, but who also teach others to do the same.

Identify five possible people to whom you could be a mentor. Possibilities include a neighborhood child, a niece or nephew, a junior employee at your workplace or a new member at your church. Pick one of those people, and identify ten mentorship opportunities for you in relationship to that person.

Next, identify and honor ten mentors in your community. Praise them less for their own accomplishments than for the accomplishments of the people they have helped. Save the best praise of all for those who help others learn to be mentors themselves.

STORIES ABOUT HEROES MENTORING OTHERS

William Wilberforce: "Mentor Others"

Brit$ritish abolitionist William Wilberforce was a man whose life was shaped strongly by the influence of his mentors. The most famous of these mentors was John Newton, a former slave captain turned anti-slavery crusader. Less famous, but equally influential was John Thornton, the half-brother of Wilberforce's aunt. Although he was a wealthy man, Thornton lived a plain and frugal life, and devoted the majority of his fortunes to charity. He was also a man with a good understanding of mentorship, as shown by a story that Wilberforce retold for the rest of his life.

It began one day when the young Wilberforce received an unexpected gift from Thornton, a sum of money in an amount much greater than that which would normally be entrusted to a boy of Wilberforce's age, together with a note indicating that he was to use the money on behalf of the poor. Proud of the trust Thornton had placed in him, Wilberforce dedicated the money to several local charities, and in doing formed the beginnings of what would be a lifelong habit of generosity. Thornton had well understood the lesson that children learn by doing. Merely hearing about the value of charity or watching his relatives give away money of their own would not have been enough to form the same habits in Wilberforce. In being guided to give, however, he learned first hand the satisfactions available from doing the right thing.

Years later, proof of how deeply Thornton's lessons had sunk in was provided during a time of national economic crisis, when Wilberforce personally gave away the equivalent of hundreds of thousands of dollars *more* than his entire yearly income in the form of aid to the hungry.

> *Nothing gives a greater tincture to the Mind or Morals of Man than either the good or bad Qualities possessed by those with whom they associate. A Person by being very intimate with another and being constantly in his Company naturally imbibes his Manners, and the same Sentiments occur to him…*
>
> William Wilberforce, *William Wilberforce* (Furneaux)

Geoffrey Griffin: "Mentor Others"

When Kenyan educator Geoffrey Griffin first began what would become the Starehe Boys' Centre and School, he founded it upon an ethic of mentorship. Later, as the school became larger and more organized, that ethic was formalized through the creation of a system of "Prefects." A prefect is an older student within the English system of schools who takes on a position of authority over his or her classmates. At Starehe, however, the prefect system has been altered in a way that accords with the teachings of Jesus.

Exemplifying the principles of Christian Mentorship, Starehe's system capitalizes on the natural competitive instinct of the students with a developed hierarchy of merit, a ladder of service that can be climbed towards the top position, Captain of the School. The entry-level position can be considered to include all the boys of the school, who are each expected to contribute to the administration and the upkeep of the school in some manner (typically through chores such as cleaning the dormitories or classrooms). The next level is "Sub Prefect," where a student is given additional responsibilities as an assistant in relationship to a single given location, such as the Library or the Dining Hall. Those who do well in this regard are advanced to the position of "House Prefect." The House Prefects help maintain school discipline, enforce school rules, and organize the chores and duties performed by ordinary students.

Over the House Prefects are a smaller number of "School Prefects." At this level, each School Prefect's primary responsibility is to mentor, nurture and organize the House Prefects that fall directly beneath him. The School Prefect positions include the following: House Captain (in charge of a particular dormitory), Captain of Games (in charge of the sports program), Chief Librarian, Chapel Prefect (in charge of the religious program), and Environmental Prefect (in charge of keeping the school clean and well-maintained). Above the House Prefects are two "Deputy School Captains", and finally the Head Boy or "Captain of the School," whose main job is to support, organize and mentor the School Prefects, and to assist them in the completion of their duties.

In the original English version of the prefect system, the authority held by students is often abused. Like a corrupt policeman, the prefect in an English school is likely to be a bully with a badge. Aggravating the situation is the fact that many schools give special privileges to the prefects that set them apart from their fellow classmates. In an earlier era, these privileges even included the power to administer corporal punishments (canings or beatings) to other students, which made the prefects figures of fearful respect in the school.

At Starehe, in contrast, the only special privilege advanced to a prefect is an increased opportunity to be of service to the school. Those who seek the position are thus motivated not by the opportunity to wield power over their classmates, but rather by the opportunity to serve. In addition Starehe prefects are never chosen strictly because of their age or grade level. No one is promoted automatically to the position of prefect as a result of having been at the school longer. Similarly, no prefect is elected to the office solely because of popularity among his peers; nor is any appointed to the office by the administration because he is a "teacher's pet" or a favorite of the administration. Instead, each prefect must be affirmed jointly by the students and the staff.

A final safeguard is the fact that the prefect position can never be considered absolutely secure. While every attempt is made to retain an appointed prefect, anyone who fails to uphold their responsibilities, abuses their position, or begins to fall behind in his classwork is quietly returned to the status of an ordinary student.

As a result of its structure, the Starehe system of prefects functions so smoothly that the majority of the non-academic tasks at the school are entrusted entirely into its care. This is essential given Starehe's unique nature. As a school serving mostly destitute students in an impoverished country, it is important for the school to maximize all available resources.

Generally, the administration of a boarding school is very complex, and potentially very expensive, particularly in the form of administrative salaries. At Starehe, however, everything outside of the classroom is administrated primarily by the prefects. For example, there is no janitorial staff. Instead, the gleaming cleanliness of the school is maintained entirely by the students under the direction of the prefect system.

Similarly, the 80 person dormitories, the 1000 person dining hall, and the 33,000 book school library are also run through the prefect system, with little or no need for input from adults. The fiscal savings to the school are enormous, but more importantly, the boys learn to take pride and ownership in their surroundings. Because of this, vandalism, graffiti, and even littering are unknown in the school. Since the students themselves are the caretakers of the grounds, they avoid doing anything that might increase their own workload, or the workload of their fellow students.

The true reward of a Prefect is the chance to give service to his School... Carved above the door of our Hall is the biblical dictum "From those to whom much has been given, much will be required." Perhaps the most important of all the lessons that any boy can learn at school is that when you receive most, you must also give most...

Geoffrey Griffin, *School Mastery*

CLOSING PRAYER (*inspired by* Matthew 10:1, John 13:15, 34)

Dear Lord, help me; help me to help others; and help me to help others help others. Amen.

MAXIMIZE YOUR RESOURCES

Therefore I say unto you, Take no thought for your life, what you shall eat; neither for the body, what you shall wear.
Life is more than food, and the body is more than clothing. Consider the ravens: for they neither plant nor harvest; they neither have storehouse nor barn; and God feeds them: And how much better are you than the birds!

And which of you can add one inch to his height through willpower? If you are not able to do that which is least, why worry about the rest?

Consider the lilies, how they grow: they neither work nor spin, and yet I tell you that Solomon in all his glory was not clothed as richly as one of them. If God so clothes the grass, which is today in the field, and tomorrow is cast into the oven; how much more will he clothe you, O you of little faith?

And do not seek what you shall eat, or what you shall drink, neither be you of doubtful mind. For all these things are sought by those of every nation, and your Father knows that you have need of these things. But rather seek the kingdom of God; and all these things shall be added unto you.

Fear not, little flock; for it is your Father's desire to give you the kingdom. Sell what you have, and give to charity; provide yourselves containers that will not decay, a treasure in the heavens that will not fail, that no thief can come near, and no moth can destroy. For where your treasure is, there also will be your heart.

Luke 20:22-34

One of Jesus' most striking and pointed parables is about a farmer who has a particularly good year. His fields are overflowing with produce to the point where he can no longer even store everything he has harvested. In a mood of cheerful self-congratulation, he decides to tear down his old barns, and build new barns that will be twice as large. By doing this, he plans to save enough that he can enjoy himself in peace, comfort and security for many years to come.

Unfortunately, in the midst of his plenty, he hears a voice from heaven. "Fool! This very night, your soul will be required of you, and then who will enjoy all your wealth?" Like so many people in modern times, the farmer of the parable believed that his savings and investments would provide him a happy retirement. His own death, however, was right around the corner, and his trust in material success turned out to be misplaced.

The lesson for Christian Heroes, and the communities they lead, is to not hoard their resources. Rather, everything that your community has should be put to its best possible use at all times. A Christian Hero does not waste anything he or she owns, nor hoard anything he or she does not use. As Jesus made clear, God will call us to account for the resources we hoard and opportunities we waste.

This lesson has particular relevance for the Christian Hero of today and now, in light of the environmental crises produced by our society's wasteful ways. Back in chapter nine, we examined the parable of the talents; the story of two good servants who increased what was entrusted them by their lord, and one bad servant who wasted the opportunity he was given. We must learn to see the environmental resources of the world —the fresh water, the vast forests, the fertile oceans, the deposits of oils, minerals and metal –as all having been entrusted to us by God in the exact same way as the money was entrusted to the three servants by their Lord in the parable of the talents. As we recall, when the Lord of the parable returned, he praised the servants who had done well with their resources, and chastised the servant who had done poorly with his. We people of today, however, are in even more danger than the unprofitable servant. He at least buried his resources and was able to return to his Lord exactly as much as he had been given. We, on the other hand, are squandering our resources so quickly that we are in real danger of being left with none of what was entrusted to us at all.

Take an inventory of all the things that you own or your community owns. Each item on the list should be in use. If not, either figure out a way to use it, or find a way to donate it to a person or community who will be able to use it. For everything that is being used, consider whether you are using it as fully and as well as possible. Consider money, space, human resources and environmental resources, as well as any other kind of resources you can identify.

HEROES MAXIMIZING RESOURCES

Martin Luther King, Jr.:
"Maximize Your Resources"

Martin Luther King, Jr. was often forced to be creative because of being denied the resources and opportunities of mainstream society. This ability to maximize his resources became a crucial part of the success of the Montgomery bus boycott.

At the start, the segregationists of Montgomery believed the boycott was doomed to failure because most black people in the city were dependent on public transportation, and there was no other means of transport available. Instead of giving up, however, King and the other blacks of Montgomery used every available resource at their disposal. Those fortunate to have cars of their own organized car-pools, sometimes shuttling multiple car-loads of passengers between one place and another. Others used their powers of persuasion to secure rides from their white employers, even when those same employers favored segregation. Finally, when all else failed, the blacks of Montgomery went from place to place on foot, even when that took many extra hours, and resulted in weary and aching feet.

As a result of their resourcefulness, the blacks of Montgomery proved they could and would live in independence from the bus system. In the end, the bus boycott was a success largely because the city of Montgomery was more dependent on the resources represented by its black citizens than those citizens were dependent on the resources offered them by their city.

> Where can we store our goods? Again the answer is simple: we can store our surplus food free of charge in the shriveled stomachs of the millions of God's children who go to bed hungry at night. We can use our vast resources of wealth to wipe poverty from the earth.
> Martin Luther King, Jr. "The Man Who Was a Fool", *Strength to Love*

Mother Teresa: "Maximize Your Resources"

Although their family was not poor, Mother Teresa's mother, Drana, believed that thriftiness was a virtue. In their house, even the electric lights would not be turned on at night unless there was productive work being done in the household.

In her later life as a nun, Mother Teresa took her mother's philosophy of thrift and applied it to every part of her organization. As a result of her ability to maximize her resources, she was able to open new programs, homes and projects in a matter of months, where others might have taken years to plan and implement each detail. By forcing each project to subsist on a minimum of funding, Mother Teresa was able to spread her resources as widely and as effectively as possible.

Even on the occasion of receiving the Nobel Peace Prize, Mother Teresa kept this philosophy very much in mind. When she found out that the Prize Committee was intending to throw her a reception costing $6000, she instead asked for the money, and used it to buy an entire year's worth of food for 400 people within her homes. Similarly, when Pope Paul VI gave her a luxury car, she immediately raffled it off, and used the money to open a leper's colony.

How can you truly know the poor unless you live like them? If they complain about the food, we can say that we eat the same. The more we have the less we can give. Poverty is a wonderful gift because it gives us freedom —it means we have fewer obstacles to God.

Mother Teresa

Sundar Singh: "Maximize Your Resources"

Sádhu Sundar Singh grew up in the lap of luxury, in the home of a wealthy family. It was perhaps the emptiness and unhappiness he felt there, in the midst of plenty, that convinced him that he needed no other resources in life than what he gained through service to Christ. Accordingly, he spent the next forty years of his life both homeless and penniless; carrying only the Bible; wearing only his *sádhu's* robes; eating only what was given to him, or what he could find; taking shelter only as it was offered; and traveling from place to place either on foot, or by transportation arranged by his supporters. In spite of these restrictions he maximized his resources in a way that allowed him to travel worldwide, and to touch the lives of many thousands of people.

Many people are surprised to see me in my simple dress with no socks or boots on my feet. But I told them that I love simplicity and that wherever I go I want to live in the same way as I live in India, not changing my color like a chameleon. I have been in England only two weeks and so cannot speak with much confidence of my impressions. But I feel that, just as the sun is seldom to be seen on account of fogs and mist, so the Sun ["Son"] of Righteousness is almost always hidden by the fogs and mists of materialism.
Sundar Singh, *The Message of Sádhu Sundar Singh* (Streeter)

Mahalia Jackson: "Maximize Your Resources"

Gospel singer Mahalia Jackson was known for being thrifty and tight with money. She could also, however, be surprisingly generous, and she knew well how to maximize her resources by making a small amount of money travel a large distance.

For example, one night during the middle of the Great Depression, Jackson was traveling home from work when she saw a large group of people standing in a soup line. At the time, Jackson had yet to strike it rich, and she was supporting herself not only through her music, but with a second job doing laundry. Even with so little in her own pocket, however, she was acutely aware of how many others were doing even worse. Accordingly, she invited the people she saw standing there home to her house, even though they were strangers to her. There she fed them a good home-cooked meal, thrown together from what odds and ends she could find around the house. At the end of the meal, her guests were so grateful that Jackson decided to make it a regular occurrence. Just as the disciples of Christ had witnessed on the occasion of the miracle of the loaves and fishes, Jackson had discovered that a little could go a long way when shared in a spirit of love.

> I just told a bunch of those guys to come on over to my house and I cooked string beans, and ham hocks and cornbread, and neck bones and rice. I must have fed about twenty people.
> Mahalia Jackson, *The Voice of Gospel and Civil Rights* (Kramer)

Toyohiko Kagawa: "Maximize Your Resources"

Few people have ever carried the principle of maximizing every resource to as extreme lengths as Reverend Toyohiko Kagawa of Japan. During his years in seminary he took the meager allowance the students were given for living expenses, and devoted it to serving the poor. Although his fellow students found it difficult to support even themselves on the minimal scholarship, Kagawa found a way to get the most out of every last yen.

His first move was to leave the student dormitory. The small private rooms there were simple and plain, but even so, Kagawa found them overpriced and self-indulgent. Instead he elected to move into one of the city's poorest slums, where real estate was cheap. Once there, he found the best possible price by renting a hovel that had been abandoned for many years because it had a reputation for being haunted.

Once he had changed locations, Kagawa also simplified his meals, electing to subsist chiefly on twice-daily rations of rice and water. In this manner, he was able to cut his expenses down to the minimum necessary for survival.

His goal, however, was neither simply to save money, nor, like the medieval monks, to suffer for the purpose of suffering. Instead, his plan was to spread his scant funds as widely as possible. By offering his own food and shelter to the homeless and the destitute of the neighborhood, he was able to support four adults on the equivalent of ten and a half American dollars a month, an amount that was considered barely adequate for a single person alone. When donations increased his income to fifty dollars a month, he increased his household size to sixteen.

Throughout life, Kagawa maintained his determination to help as many people as possible with his every available resource. Even when he had a wife and three children of his own to support, he still devoted the overwhelming bulk of his income to his numerous programs for the poor. By the time of his death, his efforts and his initiatives had touched the lives of millions throughout Japan.

> *If you want to live a happy life, make it simple. The sense of beauty does not come from luxurious living. The beauty of art and nature is in its simplicity, and it is only by living in simplicity that we can learn the beauty of God.*
> Toyohiko Kagawa, *A Seed Shall Serve* (Simon)

CLOSING PRAYER (*inspired by* Mark 12:41-44)

Dear Lord, help me use everything you have given me to its fullest extent, Amen.

INVEST IN PEOPLE

Jesus, walking by the Sea of Galilee, saw two fishermen, Simon called "Peter", and Andrew his brother, casting a net into the sea. And Jesus said to them, "Follow me, and I will make you fishers of men." And they immediately left their nets, and followed him.

Matthew 4:18-20

Jesus had the ability to see those around him not as they were at the moment, but as the amazing people they could become. For example, when everyone else saw a corrupt and greedy tax collector, Jesus saw Matthew, a great evangelist. When everyone else saw a woman possessed by demons, Jesus saw Mary Magdalene, one of his most important disciples. When everyone else saw Simon, an ignorant fisherman, Jesus saw Peter, the rock on which he would found his church.

In the same way, the Christian Hero must learn to see people with the vision of Jesus, and to love them, nurture them and invest in them in the way that Jesus loved, nurtured, and invested in his disciples. As Jesus said, God sends gifts of sun and rain to all people, whether good or bad. Accordingly, if you wish to be a true Hero for Christ, you must give your love and your loving gifts to everyone you meet. It sounds selfless, but the rewards are many. Those same people you help today will be the ones who help your community tomorrow.

Identify five people in or near to your community who seem worthless, friendless, helpless or sinister. Find something of value in each of those people. Then, identify three ways you can support them becoming their best possible selves.

STORIES ABOUT HEROES INVESTING IN PEOPLE

Geoffrey Griffin: "Invest In People"

As dynamic a leader as was Kenyan educator Geoffrey Griffin, he would have had little success in creating his ground-breaking school, *Starehe*, without the help of two other men, Geoffrey Geturo (Gatama) and Joseph Kamiru Gikubu. The two men were involved with every facet of the school from its start to the present day, with Geturo remaining with the school until his death in 1990, and with Gikubu taking over the position of Director upon Griffin's death. The two of them were especially vital in the early days of Starehe, when Kenya was making the difficult transition from a British colony to an independent nation. During that time, any white former colonialist, such as Griffin, was viewed with suspicion, bitterness and hatred by a sizable portion of the population. The support of Geturo and Gikubu, however, helped Griffin gain crucial credibility and respect among black Kenyans.

This raises a question, however. How did Griffin first gain the respect of Geturo and Gikubu? The answer is simple. They were among the two thousand juvenile detainees whom Griffin rescued from the Manyani Prison Camp. Having recognized their leadership potential from the start, Griffin soon promoted the two former prisoners to positions of trust and authority. By investing in two boys that others had seen merely as anonymous offenders, Griffin paved the way for a lifetime of benefits paid out in the form of service to Starehe.

> *Whatever needed to be done, he did it superbly well. No matter how weak he was or how much in pain, he never stopped working… No man ever had more faithful colleague than he was to me. His work continues on earth, through the lives of nearly 9,000 boys who knew him, some at least of whom must have been touched by and will follow his example that indeed the path of duty is the way to glory.*
>
> Geoffrey Griffin, "Eulogy of Geoffrey Geturo"

Mother Teresa: "Invest In People"

Throughout her career, Mother Teresa was known for investing in people, helping them find and develop their own capacity to be instruments of God's love. The process began with the first nuns of her new order, who were all former students who had been inspired by her loving example. By the time of Mother Teresa's death, those first sisters had been joined by thousands of others around the world.

Another example of Mother Teresa's personal investments is shown by the story of Jacqueline De Decker, whom Mother Teresa met as a young Belgian social worker living in India in 1948.

Although De Decker initially wished to become one of Mother Teresa's nuns, she was prevented by her poor health. With Mother Teresa's encouragement, she founded the "Sick and Suffering Co-Workers of the Missionaries of Charity," a group of those whose health was too poor to do the physical work that the missionaries accomplished, but who provided prayers and spiritual support to their counterparts among the nuns.

A similar story began in 1954, when Mother Teresa was contacted by Ann Blaikie, a British mother of three living in Kolkata who had been inspired by Mother Teresa's work. When Blaikie asked what she could do to help, Mother Teresa asked her to join together with her friends to buy Christmas presents for local orphans. Blaikie was so inspired by the experience that she founded a group called the Marian Society. Over the course of the next year, they were able to raise enough funds to allow Mother Teresa to open Shishu Bhavan, her first children's home. Later Blaikie would go on to be the first head of the International Co-Workers of Mother Teresa, a multi-faith lay organization supporting Mother Teresa's work.

In 1964, ten years after Blaikie and Mother Teresa first met, a young Jesuit priest named Ian Travers-Ball spent a few weeks working in the same children's home that the Marian Society had made possible. Although he initially found Mother Teresa's work excessively difficult, he returned less than a year later to become the head of the Missionary of Charity Brothers, a brand-new brother organization to Mother Teresa's nuns.

At home we must love our sisters. They too are the poorest of the poor. Afterwards it will be easy outside.

Mother Teresa, *Total Surrender*

CLOSING PRAYER (*inspired by* Luke 13:6-9)

Dear Lord, allow me to be the gardener who helps your trees to bear fruit, Amen.

19

BE BOLD

Ask, and it shall be given you; seek, and you shall find; knock, and the door shall be opened. For every one that asks receives; and he that seeks finds; and to he that knocks shall the door be opened.

Luke 11:9-10

One night Jesus sent his disciples ahead of him in a ship, so that he could have some time alone to pray and meditate. Although the disciples were supposed to stay close to shore, a stormy wind blew them all the way out to the middle of the waters. Late that night, however, as the disciples watched in amazement, Jesus walked to join them, crossing across the water as though it were dry land The most astounded was Peter, who immediately asked Jesus to teach him how to do the same. In response Jesus held out a hand and summoned Peter, who began walking on the waves towards his Lord. Before he got there, however, he began to sink, and had to be rescued by Jesus, who chastised him for losing his faith.

This story marks just one of the many times within the gospels where Jesus credited faith as providing the power that makes miracles happen. Elsewhere, he famously told his disciples that all they needed was faith the size of a grain of mustard, and they would be able to move mountains. Conversely, when Jesus was near the place where he was raised, he performed few miracles, a fact which he blamed on his neighbors' lack of faith.

The lesson here for the Christian Hero is to be both bold and ambitious in doing God's work. After all, Jesus said that faith can move mountains, and not that faith can move molehills. To dream only small dreams, plan only little plans, and envision only tiny visions betrays a lack of faith. A true Hero for Christ thinks big –not selfishly, but on behalf of others –with the faith that God will make it happen.

Identify your hopes and dreams for humanity as a whole in the future. What changes in the world would make life better for everyone? What would it look like to live in a society that truly followed the teachings of Jesus?

STORIES ABOUT BOLD HEROES

William Wilberforce: "Be Bold"

British abolitionist leader William Wilberforce's successful campaign to end the involvement of Britain in the slave trade is a textbook example of how to conduct a Christian project. Appropriately, it all began with a bold vision –not a mystical experience, but a commitment to the two goals that Wilberforce would pursue for the rest of his life: the end of slavery, and the improvement of British morality.

Wilberforce had been interested in the topic of slavery for quite some time. At age twenty-one he had asked a friend who was traveling to Antigua (in the British Caribbean) to bring him back a report on the condition of the enslaved workers there. Even at that early date he was already expressing a desire to do something to right the wrongs of slavery.

Prior to his rediscovery of Christianity, however, Wilberforce was a typically distractible young man, who was immersed in the world of politics, and concerned with the affairs of everyday life. Accordingly, his interest in slavery remained largely at the level of idle curiosity. What Wilberforce himself referred to as the "Great Change" occurred sometime after his twenty-fifth birthday. As Christianity began to enter his heart he discovered a new sense of moral clarity and focus. Increasingly, he became convinced that God intended him for some great work. It was then that his attention returned to the foremost evil of his times, the willingness of Britain to embrace the horrors of slavery in exchange for financial profit. Soon he had acquired a new group of friends, a circle of activists whose faith and opposition to slavery matched his own. The final confirmation came when he went to consult his old mentor, John Newton, a former slave ship captain who had become an ardent abolitionist. A few days later, Wilberforce announced in his journal his conviction that he now knew the two tasks that God had established for his life.

At the time, the abolition of the British slave trade seemed like an impossible dream to all but the boldest enemies of slavery. Slavery was a source of considerable profit for many powerful interests within the British Empire. On the occasion of his first introduction of an abolitionist bill into Parliament, Wilberforce was met by claims that abolition would ruin the British Navy, wreck the British economy, and destroy the British Colonies. Even those who were sympathetic to his cause urged him to try instead for half-measures, such as limiting the number of slaves who could be packed onto a single ship. Instead,

Wilberforce stuck to his guns, insisting that the slave trade needed to be ended, and not merely reformed.

Later, after the prohibition of the slave trade, Wilberforce refused to rest on his laurels. Instead, he turned his attention to other bold goals, including the end of capital punishment and the formation of national protections for workers. Then, late in life, he undertook his most ambitious goal yet, the complete emancipation and release of all slaves everywhere throughout the British Colonies. As before, there were many who called his goals unreasonable. As before, however, it was Wilberforce whom history proved correct.

> *God Almighty has placed before me* two great objects, *the suppression of the slave trade and the reformation of manners [morals].*
> William Wilberforce, *A Hero For Humanity* (Belmonte)

Mother Teresa: "Be Bold"

During her first fifteen years as a nun, Mother Teresa worked quietly teaching children at a convent school. Once she left the convent to work directly with the poor, however, she never looked back. No project was too small for her to turn time and attention towards; but no project was too large for her to dream about and build towards.

Even though she was only a humble nun, she was bold enough to apply directly to the Pope for permission to start her own order. Once she began to build, her ambitions to help the poor knew no bounds. By 1965, she had applied again to the Pope for permission to establish branches of her order outside of the country. Although India had always been seen only as a place in need of missionaries, Mother Teresa reversed the equation, and sent her Sisters of Charity all around the world.

> God said to one of our sisters: "I have so many sisters like you —ordinary, good sisters; I can pave the streets with them. I want fervent ones: saints."
>
> Mother Teresa, *Total Surrender*

Martin Luther King, Jr.: "Be Bold"

The foremost visionary of modern times was Reverend Martin Luther King, Jr., who is best remembered for his "I have a dream," speech. In that speech, he outlined his God-given vision of a happier, healthier nation, freed from racial prejudice and hatred. In a time in which many people were advocating small steps forward, King was strikingly bold in his goals for the nation. When President John F. Kennedy met with him and offered some small gestures of support, King demanded nothing less that what he called a "Second Emancipation Proclamation" to end segregation nationwide. Later, when King met with President Lyndon B. Johnson, he was no less bold in his demand for immediate passage of a law protecting the rights of black voters.

Perhaps his boldest moment, however, came in his speech during the March on Washington. The march itself had already been a brave move on King's part. It was a public event unexcelled in the nation's history, bringing together in a display of peace and unity a quarter of a million people of all ages, races, and descriptions. King revealed himself, however, as yet more ambitious in his speech. Unlike the majority of his comrades, who were focused on narrower questions of legal justice and equity, King had a dream that extended down to the very roots of human nature. In defiance of every grim reality he had faced, King still believed that persons of all ethnicities could come together in perfect brotherhood, and transform the homes of the worst and most deeply entrenched prejudices into beacons of enlightenment.

And so even though we face the difficulties of today and tomorrow, I still have a dream. It is a dream deeply rooted in the American dream.
I have a dream that one day this nation will rise up and live out the true meaning of its creed: "We hold these truths to be self-evident, that all men are created equal."
...
    I have a dream today!
    I have a dream that one day, down in Alabama, with its vicious racists, with its governor having his lips dripping with the words of "interposition" and "nullification" -- one day right there in Alabama little black boys and black girls will be able to join hands with little white boys and white girls as sisters and brothers.
    I have a dream today!
    I have a dream that one day every valley shall be exalted, and every hill and mountain shall be made low, the rough places will be made plain, and the crooked places will be made straight; "and the glory of the Lord shall be revealed and all flesh shall see it together."
                                    Martin Luther King, *"I Have a Dream"*

CLOSING PRAYER (*inspired by* Mark 9:23-24)

Lord, I believe; help my unbelief. You called me into the world as an instrument of your love. Make me ambitious and effective in bringing your love into the world. Amen.

ATTEND TO THE DETAILS

He that is faithful in the smallest details is faithful in the large things: and he that is unjust in the smallest details is unjust in the large things.

Luke 16:10

One of Jesus' parables tells of a man who plants a tiny mustard seed and watches it grow into a towering tree. Another parable tells of a woman who takes a tiny bit of yeast, and uses it to leaven three vats of dough. In both parables, the message is the same. Both the seed and the yeast represent faith and the faith-guided vision. The vision starts small like the seed, but grows mighty and strong like the tree, and spreads through out the society with a transformative effect, just as the yeast spreads throughout the dough.

A third parable tells of a barren fig tree. The owner of the tree plans to cut it down, because it bears no figs, but the gardener intercedes. He tends to the tree, clearing the ground around its roots, and fertilizing it, all in the hope that it will bring forth fruit. In the same way as the gardener takes concrete steps towards the success of the tree, the Christian Hero must be prepared to take concrete steps towards the success of his or her vision. It is important never to lose sight of the larger vision, and the faith that undergirds that vision, but it is also important to attend to the small details that will enable the vision to reach fruition.

Pick one of the hopes and dreams you identified earlier as part of your vision for humanity as a whole. Identify five projects that would contribute in some way, no matter how small, towards achieving that goal. Make sure all of the projects are local, practical, and capable of immediate implementation. Select one of those projects and plan it out step-by-step. Include details such as goals and outcomes, ways to measure those outcomes, resources needed, and resources available. Then start putting the steps into action.

STORIES ABOUT HEROES
ATTENDING TO THE DETAILS

Thérèse of Lisieux: "Attend to the Details"

Saint Thérèse of Lisieux was a nun whose poor health and physical frailty prevented her from kinds of active service she might otherwise have chosen. Instead, she learned to attend to the details by making every tiny action of her daily life an expression of love for God and for those around her. According to her "Little Way" of humble service weeding a garden, scrubbing a floor, sewing a shirt, or any other daily task, no matter how mundane, can be transformed by doing it in a spirit of love. From this point of view, it is less the actions you take and more the spirit in which you take them that makes the difference. Despite her early death and unexceptional life, Saint Thérèse is one of only three women in history honored as a "Doctor of the Catholic Church."

The only way I have of proving my love is to strew flowers before Thee--that is to say, I will let no tiny sacrifice pass, no look, no word. I wish to profit by the smallest actions, and to do them for Love.
Thérèse of Lisieux, *The Story of a Soul*

William Wilberforce: "Attend to the Details"

Throughout his lengthy anti-slavery campaign British abolitionist William Wilberforce remained steadfastly committed to his undiluted larger goal of an absolute end to the slave trade. He was more than willing, however, to attend to whatever details that seemed to align with his larger mission. Thus, during the long years in which abolition failed to pass in Parliament, Wilberforce published pamphlets, founded organizations, and gave speeches, all of which played a role in changing the overall mood and attitude of the public-at-large on the issue of slavery.

Perhaps his most important concrete action, however, was to support a legal maneuver designed by James Stephen, a brilliant lawyer who also happened to be Wilberforce's brother-in-law. The plan comprised two parts. The first was to push Wilberforce's friend, Prime Minister William Pitt, to sign an executive order banning the slave trade in colonies conquered by Britain. This was accomplished, although not without difficulty, by a combination of political and personal influence.

The second part took clever advantage of a situation that Wilberforce had opposed from its very start, the involvement of Britain in the Napoleonic Wars against France. Although Wilberforce was a committed pacifist, he and his allies capitalized on the spirit of wartime patriotism by passing a bill forbidding free passage through war zones to ships flying the neutral American flag. Although the bill did offer actual military advantages, its hidden role was to give teeth to Pitt's executive order by stopping slave-trading ships from passing through the war blockade.

By de-emphasizing the underlying goal of abolition, Wilberforce's allies were easily able to pass the bill. By the time the supporters of slavery realized what had happened it was too late. Together, the executive order and the new bill cut off a substantial portion of the slave trade, and made the remainder of it unprofitable. By the time Wilberforce again introduced a bill of abolition, a brief year later, the slave trade had been severely crippled. This in turn led to a change in the political climate that allowed Wilberforce's bill to pass through Parliament with overwhelming support.

When I consider the particulars of my duty I blush at the review; but my shame is not occasioned by my thinking that I am too studiously diligent in the business of life… On the contrary, I then feel that I am serving God best when from the proper motives I am most actively engaged in it.
William Wilberforce, *A Hero For Humanity* (Belmonte)

Martin Luther King, Jr.: "Attend to the Details"

Reverend Martin Luther King, Jr., learned a hard lesson about attending to the details in Albany, Georgia. At a time when the memory of his success in the Montgomery bus boycott was still fresh in the public's mind, members of the Student Nonviolent Coordinating Committee called upon King to assist in organizing the Albany civil-rights movement. By then, local leaders had already been organizing for nearly a year around a wide list of demands for progress, including the desegregation of buses, trains, libraries, parks and hospitals, an end to police brutality and the admission of blacks onto juries.

Although the people in Albany were no less motivated or committed than those in Montgomery, and although King brought the same soul-stirring speeches and sense of moral vision with him, the Albany movement was largely a failure, at least in terms of King's involvement. In Montgomery, he and the other organizers had one big issue on which to concentrate, the desegregation of the buses. In Albany, on the other hand, the list of demands was long and unfocused. By making and breaking vague promises, and by offering concessions on one issue at the same time as denying them on another, the segregationist leadership of Albany was able to play games with the movement, while avoiding any real or substantive changes.

When King moved on to Birmingham, Alabama, he remembered the lessons learned in Albany. Instead of a vague list of demands, he and his supporters approached Birmingham with a concrete and specific set of objectives, focused squarely around integrating the businesses of Birmingham. In the end, after a long hard struggle, not only did they achieve each of their carefully articulated goals, they also progressed towards the larger social changes they had hoped for.

The mistake I made there was to protest against segregation generally rather than against a single and distinct facet of it. Our protest was so vague that we got nothing, and the people were left very depressed and in despair. It would have been much better to have concentrated upon integrating the buses or the lunch counters. One victory of this kind would have been symbolic, would have galvanized support and boosted morale.
      Martin Luther King, Jr., *The Autobiography of Martin Luther King, Jr.*

Mother Teresa: "Attend to the Details"

Mother Teresa received what she named her "Second Calling" –to leave the convent and go serve the poor directly –while recovering from a bad bout with tuberculosis. Although she was impatient to follow instructions she believed were straight from God, she decided to use her recuperative time wisely. She asked for writing utensils, and began to attend to the details of the plans for her future work. She started by describing her vision, as founded in both her original calling (to be a nun), and in her Second Calling. She then went on to describe trust, surrender and an attitude of joy as the values she wanted to embody in her work. Finally, she outlined concrete working guidelines both for herself and for those who would join her in the future. Although Mother Teresa revised and expanded her goals and methods many times over the years, the core of everything she would ever do was already present in her first formulation of her plan.

Don't waste time waiting for big things to do for God. You will not have the readiness to say yes to the great things if you do not train yourselves to say yes to the thousand-and-one occasions of obedience that come your way throughout the day.

Mother Teresa, *Total Surrender*

CLOSING PRAYER (*inspired by* Matthew 12:35)

Dear Lord, help me turn my love for you into concrete and productive action on behalf of my fellow human beings. Amen.

BE COMMITTED

And Jesus answered, saying, Martha, Martha, you are careful and troubled about many things, but one thing is necessary: and Mary has chosen that good part, which shall not be taken away from her.

Luke 10:41-42

The Gospel of Luke tells the story of a man who wanted to follow Jesus, but who asked permission to first say goodbye to his family. To the man's surprise, Jesus replied "No man who looks back after having put his hand to the plow is ready for the kingdom of God." The words seem harsh, but there is an important lesson behind them. Following God is a momentous decision. It is something to which one must fully commit, without knowing the consequences, and without doubts and second thoughts.

In addition to this first and most important commitment of life, the commitment to God, the Christian Hero must also have the willingness and the ability to commit to smaller projects and plans in pursuit of his or her faith-guided vision. This is a key part of turning faith into action. Even though any given vision could lead to many possible projects, it is not possible to work on all projects at once. Many talented people never reach their goals because they switch attention to the next project before the last one is complete. In this, they are like Jesus' disciple Martha, who was troubled about many things, when only one was important.

This is why you must choose your projects wisely. Once you have committed to a project, following it will require sacrifices of time, effort and resources. You will also be forced to set aside other worthwhile tasks so you can focus on your original project. For all these reasons, you should never commit to a project without first seeking guidance from God through spending time in prayer.

Once having made that commitment, however, you should be prepared to see the project through either until its final success, or until you receive clear indications from God that the project should be abandoned. Any other event should be treated as an obstacle than can and must be overcome.

Pick a project to which you can commit. Then list ten sacrifices you are willing to make in order to bring your project to success.

STORIES ABOUT COMMITTED HEROES

William Wilberforce: "Be Committed"

British abolitionist William Wilberforce never shied away from the sacrifices involved in being committed to the end of British slavery, even when those sacrifices involved his own personal safety. For example, in the late 1780's Wilberforce managed to compel two wealthy and powerful slave captains, Robert Norris and John Kimble, to appear before Parliament in defense of the slave trade. Once he had them there, Wilberforce systematically exposed the abuses and horrors that they promoted on their ships. Although Britain was still many years away from abolishing the slave trade itself, public opinion turned rapidly against Norris and Kimble. Wilberforce was even able to have Kimble imprisoned and tried on the charge of the murder of an enslaved woman.

The tide turned again, however, when Kimble was able to have his case thrown out of court by his powerful friends. He immediately demanded that Wilberforce give him a public apology, a huge cash settlement and a government position. When Wilberforce refused, Kimble and Norris turned to cruder methods, sending death threats and even going so far as to attempt to physically ambush Wilberforce when he was traveling. Through it all, however, Wilberforce remained resolute in his conviction that what he was doing was right, no matter who might oppose him, and no matter what risks he might run.

Almighty God, under all my weakness and uncertain prospects give me grace to trust firmly in thee, that I may not sink under my sorrows nor be disquieted with the fears of those evils which cannot without thy permission fall upon me.

William Wilberforce, *A Hero For Humanity* (Belmonte)

Geoffrey Griffin: "Be Committed"

When he was still a boy, Geoffrey Griffin, the founder of Kenya's *Starehe Boys Centre*, had a profound religious experience. It was night at his boarding school and he was doing his customary evening prayers. Suddenly he had a strong sense that God was there with him, speaking to him and showing him a vision of his future. Although the vision did not provide any exact details, it nevertheless convinced Griffin that if he found the path God wanted him to walk, his subsequent efforts would be successful.

As he grew older, it took Griffin several years and false starts to discover that his destiny was as an educator. Once he found his role in life, however, he accepted it with absolute and unwavering commitment. He forewent marriage and children, choosing instead to view his students as his children. He chose also to place his work above any social life outside of the school, and kept closer contact with Starehe's alumni than with any of his own relatives. Throughout his life he worked days that could last as long as eleven hours, and spent forty-five years as the school's Director without taking a single extended vacation.

Not only was Griffin's own commitment absolute, but he demanded similar heroic efforts of his staff –to the point that he could be uncharitable to anyone who failed to meet his high standards. A particularly telling story recounts the decision of a longtime Starehe teacher to take a position at another school in exchange for higher wages. This particular teacher had given Starehe more than one decade of exemplary service, but had become tired of scraping by on his low salary. When he tendered his resignation, however, instead of receiving a commendation for his years of devotion, he was instead chastised harshly by Griffin, who accused him of selling out the destitute students of Starehe in exchange for the other school's "dirty money."

> *It has certainly been my experience that virtually any ambition in life can be attained, provided one is determined enough. And provided too, that one is prepared to pay the price, which could be very, very heavy indeed… The price of real success, generally involved many years of overwork, coupled with the taking of innumerable risks and making of enormous, and repeated, sacrifices in terms of one's own personal relationships and pleasures.*
>
> Geoffrey Griffin, "The Power of Purpose"

CLOSING PRAYER (*inspired by* Matthew 13:44-46)

Dear Lord, everything I have is from you, and everything I own is in your hands. Help me do the work you want me to do, no matter what the costs. Amen.

BE PERSISTENT

You will be hated by all men for my sake, but he who endures to the end shall be saved.

Matthew 10:22

One day Jesus told his disciples a parable about a woman who tried to get justice from a corrupt judge. At first, the judge's only thought was to ignore her, as he had doubtlessly ignored countless others. After she harassed him day and night for months, however, he decided it would be easier to give her what she wanted than to put up with her nagging persistence.

The lesson to any potential Hero for Christ is that commitment is not enough. One must also be persistent, willing to try over and over despite failures and setbacks. This is especially true when you take on a leadership position. Most people need to hear new concepts multiple times before they embrace them. Even the best ideas may be ignored when first introduced. You must also be willing to affirm even a well-established vision over and over, no matter how committed your followers may appear. A vision that is not kept fresh in the ears and minds of those who follow it is a vision that fades and becomes forgotten.

Identify between three and ten values, virtues, principles or commitments that express the heart of your vision. Affirm them daily to yourself, and to everyone else involved in your project.

STORIES ABOUT PERSISTENT HEROES

Sundar Singh: "Be Persistent"

Indian Christian Sádhu Sundar Singh was nothing if not persistent. In particular, one mission close to his heart was his effort to preach Christianity in the land of Tibet. At that time Tibet was a Buddhist theocracy, and the reaction he received was often hostile. Nevertheless, he returned there year after year without fail, traveling always by foot, over icy and treacherous terrain, and at frequent risk of his life.

In each place where he traveled, his reception was different. In some villages the locals were welcoming; in others they were indifferent. In one village, however, he was seized by the village authorities and sentenced to death for preaching a foreign religion. As Buddhists, his accusers were forbidden to take human life, but these particular villagers had created a way around that difficulty. It was their custom to throw condemned prisoners down a dry well, and to wait for them to die on their own.

After spending three days without food or water, and surrounded by the remains of previous victims, Singh was rescued by an unknown benefactor, who lowered a rope to him, but who vanished by the time

Singh struggled to the top. Rather than escape the village in haste, however, Singh elected to be persistent rather than prudent. Accordingly, he returned to the center of the village and renewed his preaching, much to the shock of the villagers, who were greatly impressed by his miraculous escape.

> *It is easy to die for Christ. It is hard to live for Him. Dying takes only an hour or two, but to live for Christ means to die daily. During the few years of this life only I am given the privilege to serve man and Christ. If it were right for me to be in Heaven always I should have been called there, but as I am still left on earth it is my duty to work.*
> Sundar Singh, *The Message of Sádhu Sundar Singh* (Streeter)

William Wilberforce: "Be Persistent"

Perhaps the most exemplary trait possessed by British abolitionist William Wilberforce was his amazing persistence. This was a crucial part of his success in fighting slavery, given that the struggle took far longer than he could have imagined.

The first time Wilberforce introduced a bill for the abolition of the slave trade was 1791, after three years of preparation, during which time Wilberforce and his allies had made fiery speeches and presented testimony and evidence to Parliament. Nonetheless, the bill was voted down, 163 to 88. Undaunted, Wilberforce introduced the same bill a year later, with much the same result. By the time a bill ending the slave trade finally passed in 1807, Wilberforce had spent nearly twenty straight years of hard work to make it possible.

> *Justice, humanity, and sound policy prescribe our course, and will animate our efforts. Stimulated by a consciousness of what we owe to the laws of God, and the rights and happiness of man, our exertions will be ardent, and our perseverance invincible. Our ultimate success is sure; and ere long we shall rejoice in the consciousness of having delivered our country from the greatest of her crimes, and rescued her character from the deepest stain of dishonour.*
>
> *William Wilberforce, A Hero For Humanity (Belmonte)*

Martin Luther King, Jr.: "Be Persistent"

Reverend Martin Luther King, Jr. knew well the importance of persistence. In his very first campaign, desegregating the buses in Montgomery Alabama, he witnessed firsthand how important it was to be undeterred by difficulties. When the bus boycott first started, there were many who had hopes that it would achieve success quickly – perhaps as soon as three or four days after it had started. Instead, days turned into weeks, and weeks turned into months. Those who had cars of their own were spared the worst brunt of the effort, but they were few and far between. Others, ranging from the young to the elderly, daily walked what would eventually total the equivalent of hundreds of miles on foot, starting in the mild Alabama winter, continuing through the storms of spring, under the hot summer sun, and on into the sullen fall. Even when it seemed like the ordeal would never end, they kept walking, with neither despair nor complaints.

King himself learned a lesson from the brave example of those he led, and also persisted, even after being arrested, having his house bombed, and having his own father urge him to flee Montgomery and retreat to Atlanta. It was a lesson that would serve him well in later years. Even doing God's work, he experienced fewer triumphs than failures. He was a success in Montgomery and Birmingham, but a failure in Albany, St. Augustine, and Chicago. In the end, however, each failure was nothing but an occasion for him to learn and to work harder. Even on the eve of his death, he was working on behalf of another group of the least, the sanitation workers of Memphis. It is because of his refusal to give up that his dreams still live on, even after his failures have been forgotten.

> *I am not unmindful that some of you come here out of excessive trials and tribulation. Some of you have come fresh from narrow jail cells. Some of you have come from areas where your quest for freedom left you battered by the storms of persecution and staggered by the winds of police brutality. You have been the veterans of creative suffering. Continue to work with the faith that unearned suffering is redemptive.*
>
> Martin Luther King, Jr., *"I Have a Dream"*

Mother Teresa: "Be Persistent"

As soon as Mother Teresa returned to the convent after receiving her "Second Calling" she went to her spiritual director, and shared with him her dreams of serving the poor in the streets. Her spiritual director referred her to the Archbishop, who thought that her plans were too dangerous and difficult, and sent her back to the convent.

For the next year, she continued her duties as a nun, but prayed every night and day that she would receive a blessing to leave the convent. Eventually, when she felt the time was right, she went back to the Archbishop. This time, he referred her to the head of her own order, Mother Gertrude. Mother Gertrude was sympathetic to her request, but decided that what they needed was permission from the Vatican in Rome.

Next, she spent several more months waiting for her request to make its way through the church hierarchy. Eventually she received a letter containing a special permission from the Pope. Even now she still needed to go back to the Archbishop, who was in charge of all Catholics in the region. This time, with the Pope's letter in her hand, Mother Teresa was able to receive the Archbishop's blessing. He insisted, however, that she first get training as a nurse by working with the Medical Mission Sisters in Patna. By the time Mother Teresa had finished her training and returned to start her work in Kolkata, it had been over two years since she received her Second Calling. In all that time, her dreams of service had never been far from her mind. Had she not been so persistent, her dreams would never have come true.

> *To labor at the conversion and sanctification of the poor in the slums involves hard, ceaseless toiling, without results, without counting the cost...*
>
> *Don't allow anything to interfere with your love for Jesus. You belong to him. Nothing can separate you from him. That one sentence is important to remember. He will be your joy, your strength. If you hold onto that sentence, temptations and difficulties will come, but nothing will break you.*
> Mother Teresa, *Total Surrender*

CLOSING PRAYER (*inspired by* Matthew 17:19-20)

Dear Lord, give me the strength, courage and faith to bring this project to fruition, and let it be blessed in your sight. Amen.

㉓

BE OPEN MINDED

And there came a voice to him, saying
"Rise, Peter; kill, and eat."
But Peter said,
"Do not say so Lord;
for I have never eaten any thing that is impure or unclean."
And the voice spoke to him again, saying,
"Do not call impure that which God has cleansed."

Acts of the Apostles 10:13-15

According to the Acts of the Apostles, Saint Peter was praying one day on the roof of his friend's house when he fell into a trance. While in the trance he saw a vision of a cloth descending from heaven, filled with many of the foods forbidden by Jewish law as unclean and unfit for human consumption. As he gazed on the food, he heard a voice from heaven commanding him to eat. When he protested that he had always been a good Jew, who had never eaten non-kosher food, the voice commanded him not to call anything unclean that had been cleansed by God. The same exchange was repeated three times before the cloth returned to the heavens.

At first Peter was confused about the meaning of his vision. But even as he pondered, there came a knock at the door. Outside were messengers sent by a man named Cornelius, who was Roman, and thus a citizen of the hated Empire that had conquered Israel. Since Cornelius was not

Jewish, Peter, as an observant Jew, was forbidden to go to his home. Nonetheless, Peter immediately recognized that he was being shown the meaning of his vision. Accordingly he went to Cornelius's house, saying "You know it is unlawful for a Jew to keep company with a man of another nation; but God has shown me that I should not call any man common or unclean." From that time onward Peter fully supported welcoming even those who were not Jewish into the community of Christian believers.

At first, this caused a lot of confusion among the Apostles. There were many who thought the new converts should adopt the laws, customs and culture of the Jews as a precondition for becoming followers of Christ. Even Saint Peter himself wavered on the subject of whether the new Christians should submit to the practice of circumcision, which had been the primary mark of the bond between God and his people since the dawn of Jewish history. In the end, however, the Apostles realized that their most important job was to bring people to God through Christ. Everything else, no matter how important it might seem, was only a manmade barrier standing in the way.

The lesson here for the Christian Hero is to always be open minded. You must avoid inflexibility, even in the middle of committed and persistent pursuit of your faith-founded vision. If you are too strongly attached to specific objectives, you will blind yourself to the guidance and opportunities that God sends your way. This is a particular danger for anyone who wishes to serve as a leader.

Instead, we should be "like children," and thus truly open to God's guidance. In other words we must be utterly trusting; ready to abandon all preconceptions, prejudices and prior plans upon the instructions of our divine Parent.

Identify five issues that you feel strongly about. In regards to each one, consider as openly as you can whether you might be wrong about your convictions.

STORIES ABOUT OPEN MINDED HEROES

William Wilberforce: "Be Open Minded"

British abolitionist William Wilberforce understood the importance of being open to God's guidance, even when it ran counter to his own instincts. The most important instance of this in his life took place right at the beginning of his campaign against slavery. At the time he was a young politician who had just rediscovered faith in Christianity after a long period living the life of a worldly playboy.

His first instinct was to give up the dirty world of politics entirely, to leave London and retire to the country; and there to spend his time in prayer and meditation. He even contemplated entering the ministry, or devoting his life to some similar form of Christian service. Fortunately, however, Wilberforce's friends and mentors were united in their opinion that Wilberforce had already found the work to which God was calling him. His gift for politics was clear, and the potential for him to do good in that role was enormous.

In the end, after much prayer and soul-searching, Wilberforce decided his friends were right. He would stay on in Parliament, but as a new and different person. Where he had previously pursued his own ambitions, he would henceforward be a voice for righteousness, an advocate of the poor and the oppressed.

> I withstood with all my energy [the] counsel [that] Mr. Wilberforce… retire from public life… Had that counsel been followed, the slave trade might have been continued to future generations.
> Thomas Scott, *William Wilberforce: A Hero For Humanity* (Belmonte)

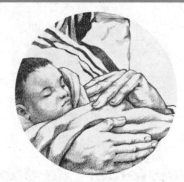

Mother Teresa: "Be Open Minded"

When Mother Teresa first planned out her new order she was devoted to the idea that her nuns would live in exactly the same manner as the poor whom they would serve. She felt it was important that there be nothing that separated or distinguished those giving the service from those being served. Accordingly, when she was training under the Medical Mission Sisters, she proudly informed Mother Dengel, the head of the order, that her new nuns would wear only simple saris and sandals, sleep on mattresses on the floor, and eat only rice and salt, which was the only food available to many of India's poor. Mother Teresa's words horrified Mother Dengel. She knew because of her medical training that anyone who ate only rice and salt would suffer from malnutrition and vitamin deficiency. Not only would their diet make Mother Teresa's nuns too weak to serve the poor, but some of them were likely to die.

At first Mother Teresa was reluctant to give up her vision of an order of nuns who would live exactly as did the poor. Eventually, however, she realized the good sense of what the older nun was telling her. By being open minded enough to give up the conceit of starving in the same way as the poor were starving, Mother Teresa saved her larger goal of service to those in need.

> *One of our brothers loves the lepers… He said to me, "I love the lepers; I want to be with them. I want to work for them. My vocation is to be with the lepers." I said to him. "Brother, you are making a mistake. Your vocation is not to work for the lepers. Your vocation is to belong to Jesus. The work for the lepers is only your love for Christ in action…"*
>
> Mother Teresa, *Total Surrender*

Toyohiko Kagawa: "Be Open Minded"

When Reverend Toyohiko Kagawa began his time in the slums of Kobe, he had no thought of ever getting married. He was committed to a life of simple poverty, and utterly devoted to his work with the poor. Not only did he have nothing in the way of material comfort to offer a wife, but he was also convinced that love could only be a distraction from his service to God.

It was with distress, therefore, that he realized his developing feelings for a young woman who had been impressed by his work, and who had started coming on a daily basis to help him tend to the needs of the sick and the homeless. He even went so far as to write a poem expressing his confusion:

> *Love, linger not to whisper your temptation,*
> *Seek not to bind me with your heavy chain*
> *I would be free to seek the world's salvation*
> *I would be free to rescue men from pain.*
>
> Toyohiko Kagawa, *A Seed Shall Serve* (Simon)

For her part, the young woman, Haru, was also developing romantic feelings towards the man whose work she admired so strongly. She was an uneducated woman from a working-class family, however, and felt that she was unworthy to consider herself as a potential mate for Kagawa, who was well-educated and from an upper-class home.

With them both having reasons to resist their emotions, their relationship might forever have remained that of two people united solely by their devotion to the poor. Things moved towards a crisis, however, when Haru's family arranged for her to marry a local teacher. It was a chance for Haru to gain a secure future, and to pursue her lifelong dream of gaining an education, yet she knew her heart was in the slums with Kagawa.

Eventually, she gathered the courage to ask Kagawa himself for advice. Should she marry a man she hardly knew and did not love; or should she stay with her work in the slums, even at the price of an uncertain future, and a rapidly fading chance of ever finding a husband?

"What do you want to do?" asked Kagawa.

"I would rather stay with you," answered Haru, "even as a lowly servant in your house."

Kagawa was deeply moved as he realized the depth of Haru's devotion to him and to their work. Although he had always believed he needed to be free of romance in order to serve God more fully, he now realized that God had a different path planned for him. His faith convinced him that he needed to be open minded enough to accept the gift that God had sent into his life. Accordingly, he told Haru that she could stay with him, not as a servant, but as his wife.

It was now Haru's turn to be open minded enough to let go of her preconceptions. Although she had often dreamed of marriage to Kagawa, she was still convinced of her own unworthiness as compared to a man she viewed as nearly a saint. After spending time in prayer, however, she too realized that everything was unfolding in accordance with God's larger plan. She accepted Kagawa's proposal and the two of them were married less than a month later. A few years later, with Kagawa's support, she was able to realize her dream of education by attending a Women's Seminary. For almost fifty years, until Kagawa's death in 1960, the two of them were each other's greatest joy and strongest support, raising three children, and remaining steadfast in their devotion to the poor.

If only we could learn to love one another, it would be a solution to our problems.

Toyohiko Kagawa

CLOSING PRAYER (*inspired by* Matthew 13:15-17)

Lord, open my eyes that I might see you, my ears that I might hear you, and my heart that I might be open to your guidance and will. Amen.

(24)

BE READY

The kingdom of heaven shall be compared to ten maidens, who took their lamps, and went forth to meet the bridegroom. And five of them were wise, and five were foolish. The foolish took their lamps without any oil, but the wise took oil in containers along with their lamps. When the bridegroom was slow in arriving, they all fell asleep. At midnight, the cry went out "Behold, the bridegroom arrives, go out to meet him!"

Then all the maidens woke up and trimmed their lamps, and the foolish said to the wise, "Give us your oil, for our lamps have gone out."

But the wise answered, "No, for there is not enough for both of us, so instead, go and buy more."

While they were buying oil, the bridegroom came, and those that were ready went in with him to the wedding, and the door was shut. And afterwards the other maidens came, saying "Lord, Lord, open the door for us." But he answered, saying "Truly I tell you, I do not know you."

Watch therefore, for you know neither the day nor the hour when the Son of Man shall come.

Matthew 25:1-13

One of Jesus' parables tells the story of a man who found a treasure in a field. Without hesitation, he immediately sold every possession he owned in order to buy the field. He knew that nothing he owned was as valuable as what he had found, and that any indecision on his part might result in someone else getting there first. Another parable tells the story of a collector of pearls who traded away everything in order to obtain a single perfect pearl. With his trained eye and obsession for pearls, he knew he could live a thousand years and never again find the pearl's equal.

The gospels tell us that the first time Simon Peter and his brother Andrew saw Jesus, they were fishing, but when Jesus called them, they left their nets full of fish and followed; without knowing where he was going, or whether they would ever return. The same was true of James and John, the sons of Zebedee, who abandoned not only their nets and their fish, but their boat and their father as well. In general, Jesus' most treasured apostles were ordinary people who abandoned everything and followed Jesus with only a moment's notice, and without any hesitation.

The last step for turning faith into action is to be ready for opportunities as they come. This is possible only if you have completed all other steps first. In other words, you must have a righteous and ambitious vision, you must be fully committed to it, you must have pursued it persistently in concrete and specific ways, and yet have been open to the guidance of God. It is then and only then that you will be willing, ready and able to take decisive action at a moment's notice.

As Jesus tells us, doing God's work involves constant vigilance and preparation for events that may come without warning. A Hero for Christ must be sure enough in his or her beliefs to take necessary actions without doubts or hesitation.

Identify five things keeping you from being ready to do God's work. Come up with a plan for overcoming each of the five, and put it into action.

STORIES ABOUT READY HEROES

William Wilberforce: "Be Ready"

The years 1805-1807 were not easy ones for British abolitionist William Wilberforce. In 1805 he had been forced once again by his conscience to take a public stand against his close friend Prime Minister William Pitt after a high ranking member of Pitt's government was accused of corruption. Then, less than a year later, Pitt died unexpectedly at the age of forty-seven. Not only did this rob Wilberforce of his one-time closest friend, it meant the simultaneous loss of his most powerful political ally. To make matters worse, Pitt's successor to the position of Prime Minister of Britain was Lord Grenville, a man whom Wilberforce personally disliked and who was known to dislike Wilberforce in turn.

Nevertheless, Grenville was a known opponent of slavery, and Wilberforce sensed that the time was right for another attack on the slave trade, despite the tragedy of Pitt's loss and the resulting political turmoil that both Wilberforce and the nation of Britain had endured. Accordingly, he and Grenville agreed to bury their personal animosity and to work together to end the slave trade in Britain, once and for all. This time, unlike in previous years, the public mood was with them, and the bill passed with overwhelming support. As unready to continue the fight as Wilberforce might have felt personally during that moment of his life, he was nonetheless politically and spiritually ready, and thus achieved the victory.

> *Pray for us, my dear sir, that we also may be enabled to hold on our way, and at last to join with you in the shout of victory… I shall ever reckon it the greatest of all my temporal favours that I have been providentially led to take the conduct of this business.*
> *William Wilberforce, A Hero For Humanity* (Belmonte)

Martin Luther King, Jr.: "Be Ready"

When Reverend Martin Luther King, Jr., left his house on December 5, 1955, he had no idea his life was about to change forever. It was true that he had recently become involved as an organizer of the new bus boycott in Montgomery, but as yet he viewed himself only as one among many.

When he arrived at that evening's meeting, he found himself surrounded by the established leaders of the community. Nearly all of them were older than he was, they had all been in Montgomery much longer, and some of them had been active in civil-rights organizing for years. There was no reason for King to believe that he would be needed or called upon for any special role in the boycott. To his surprise, however, as soon as nominations were called for, his name was put forward. It was swiftly seconded, and King found himself voted into office as the head of the new protest organization in a matter of minutes. Although he was by nature suited to a quiet life, although his election took him unawares, and although he had only recently declined an offer to run for the head of the NAACP, some part of King was ready for the demands of history and his own personal destiny. "I accept," he said.

As a minister, I am often given promises of dedication. Instinctively I examine the degree of sincerity. The striking quality in Negro students I have met is the intensity and depth of their commitment. I am no longer surprised to meet attractive, stylishly dressed young girls whose charm and personality would grace a junior prom and to hear them declare in unmistakably sincere terms, "Dr. King, I am ready to die if I must."
  Martin Luther King, Jr., "The Time for Freedom Has Come," *I have a Dream*

CLOSING PRAYER (*inspired by* Luke 12:40)

Dear Lord, grant that I be ready when you call me. Amen.

㉕

DO NOT RESIST
EVIL PERSONS

You have heard it said,
"An eye for an eye, and a tooth for a tooth:"
But I say unto you, "Do not resist those who do evil."

Matthew 5:39

Of all the mysterious, challenging and difficult to
understand things Jesus ever said, one of the most
mysterious, most challenging, and most difficult to
understand is his instruction at the center of the Sermon on
the Mount, "Do not resist those who do evil." On the surface,
it seems a contradiction of everything Christianity stands for;
and a surrender to the forces of darkness. On closer
examination, however, it reveals a core of profound and
powerful wisdom.

Too often, when we resist evil persons, we do so at the
price of becoming more like those we resist. We take up our
adversary's weapons and in doing so, we remake ourselves in
our adversary's image. Furthermore, by spending our time
and efforts responding to the work of evildoers, we lose our
chances to make progress towards better aims. In this way,
responding to an adversary is a distraction at best, and a
trap at worst.

On the other hand, a Christian Hero must never remain
passive, watching from the background as evil gains in
strength and power. Rather, a Christian Hero must take an
active role, not in resistance to those who are evil, but in

support of those who are good. He or she must tirelessly pursue a brighter future in accordance with the teachings of Jesus.

When you support good aims rather than resist evil ones, it means that you take the initiative, thus forcing those who are against you to respond to you and your goals instead of the other way around. This is a distinction that can be hard to understand, particularly in times of war. Yet war is a prime example of how resistance to evil can breed more evil. The true adversary of humanity is not any one race, nation or culture of people. Rather, it is the impulse towards violence itself, the willingness to harm or kill another human being. Each day that I fight against my brother is a victory for evil, no matter which side wins or loses any given battle.

Identify three evils in the world that bother you. Instead of concentrating merely on ways to stop them, think about things you can do to create positive changes in the same general area.

STORIES ABOUT HEROES NOT RESISTING

Mother Teresa: "Do Not Resist Evil Persons"

The proof of Mother Teresa's mastery of Jesus' technique of not resisting evildoers is that it is difficult to think of her as having enemies at all. Although she often encountered obstacles in her life and work, and although she came in for her fair share of criticism over the years, there is no evidence that she ever viewed another human being as her enemy or her adversary.

For example, consider the case of Communist dictator Enver Hoxha, who ruled for many years over Mother Teresa's homeland of Albania. An avowed Marxist atheist, he persecuted the religious, and did his best to stamp out all religion in Albania. Furthermore, his government kept Mother Teresa's own mother and sister captive in Albania, with the result that she was unable to be reunited with them before their deaths, or even to attend their funerals. If there were anyone in the world Mother Teresa would have had good cause to hate, it would have been Hoxha. Nevertheless, after his death, she made it a point to place a wreath upon his grave.

For another example, Mother Teresa came under intense criticism in the media near the end of her life –in a large part because of her perceived friendships with figures such as Hoxha's widow, the dictatorial Duvaliers of Haiti, and the embezzlers Charles Keating and Robert Maxwell. When asked to respond to her attackers, however, her only comment was that she planned to continue with her work. In that way, she refused to allow negativity to prevent her from bringing good into the world. In the end, the good that Mother Teresa did has outlasted the evils committed by Hoxha, just as her reputation as a servant to humanity will outlast the complaints lodged against her by her critics.

No matter who says what, you should accept it with a smile and do your own work.

Mother Teresa

Sundar Singh: "Do Not Resist Evil Persons"

Like Mother Teresa, Indian Christian Sádhu Sundar Singh had critics but no real enemies. The main reason was his determination to fully live out one of the most difficult of all Christ's proscriptions, against the resistance of evil persons. At various points in his life, Singh was poisoned, thrown down a well, and attacked with sticks and stones, all because of his determination to preach the word of Christ. On no occasion did he respond in kind, or even in defense of himself. Rather, prayer was his only refuge. Because of his inner calm, many of those who initially wished to attack him were instead converted to his beliefs.

For example, on one occasion he was passing through the woods near Bhulera, in the center of India. Four men attacked him as he passed, with one coming towards him with a knife. Thinking that his end had come, Singh bowed his head and waited to be struck. This action was so unexpected that it caused his assailants to hesitate. Although they had originally planned to murder him and strip his body, they decided to be satisfied with his possessions. Then, after searching him and finding no money, they let him go. Yet before he could make it very far, he was overtaken by one of thieves who called him back. Having recognized Singh's robes as those of a holy man, the robber wished to know who he was and what was his teaching. Upon being given this opportunity, Singh opened his Bible, and preached the parable of the rich man and Lazarus, with such persuasion that the thief was persuaded to repent of his wicked ways.

If we resist evil men, who would do us harm, then neither part is likely to be profited; probably both will be injured, as in the collision of two trains both are shattered. But if, by not resisting, we suffer, then, on the one hand, the cross-bearer is benefited spiritually, and on the other hand, the oppressor will be impressed by the forgiving spirit, and will be inclined towards the truth. It has been shown that by treatment of this kind the lives of many wicked men have been changed. Here is an example.

Last year, in the hills in India, while a godly Indian Christian was praying in his house alone, three thieves stealthily entered his room, and took away all they could get. When the man had finished his prayers he noticed that all his goods had gone, except the box over which he had been bowing in prayer. This box contained money and valuables. This "man of prayer" took some cash and valuables in his hands, and ran after the thieves, calling, "Wait! Wait! You have left some valuables behind. I have brought them to you. Perhaps you need these things more than I." When the thieves, heard this, at first they thought it was a trap, but when they saw that he had no weapon and that he was alone, they came back to him.

The man said to him, "Why did you not tell me at first that you needed these things? I would have gladly given you whatever I have; now you had better come home with me, and whatever you want you may take away." The thieves, seeing the strange life of this man of prayer, were so affected that their lives were changed forever and they began to say, "We never imagined that there were such people in the world. If you are so wonderful, then how much more wonderful must be your Savior, Who has made you into such a wonderful and godlike character." There we have the result of not resisting the evil.

Sundar Singh, *The Search After Reality*

CLOSING PRAYER (*inspired by* Matthew 26:52)

Dear Lord, grant that I never be tempted to resist evil with the weapons that evil has made. Amen.

(26)

LOVE GENEROUSLY

You have heard it said
"Love your neighbor, and hate your enemy."
But I say to you
"Love your enemies, bless them that curse you,
do good to those that hate you,
and pray for those who exploit you and persecute you;
that you might be the children of your Father which is in heaven;
for he makes his sun rise on the evil and on the good,
and sends the gift of rain both to the just and to the unjust."
Matthew 5:43-45

One of Jesus' most often repeated parables tells of the misadventures of a wasteful young man. This youth was so greedy that he took the unheard-of step of demanding his inheritance from his father while the old man was still alive. Then, loaded down with his share of the family's wealth, he sailed off for a foreign country, where he wasted every cent he owned on alcohol and prostitutes.

After he had burned through his inheritance, the young man was reduced to tending pigs for a share of the scraps they were fed. It was then and only then that his thoughts turned to the home and family he had scorned and left behind. Although he dreaded returning to the shame and disapproval he was sure awaited him, he finally realized that even the lowliest hired man on his father's estate had a better life than the one he now lived. Accordingly, he decided to return, even if only to be a servant in his father's home. When he arrived, however, to his surprise he was welcomed back by his father with open arms, a celebratory feast, and judgment neither for his misdeeds nor for his poor decisions.

Another parable, no less well-known, tells of a man who was overtaken by thieves while traveling. After being robbed and stripped of his clothing and belongings, the man was beaten and left for dead. As he lay there, naked and wounded at the side of the road, he was passed first by a priest, and then by a Levite, but neither man stopped to help. At length, however, a man of the Samaritan people came by on the same road. Although the Samaritans and the Jews were hereditary enemies, who hated and despised each other, the Samaritan stopped to help a fellow human being in distress. He tended to the victim's wounds, placed him on his own donkey, and paid for his lodging and care.

Many lessons can be taken from this pair of parables, but one of the most important for the Christian Hero to learn is the importance of loving generously. In the case of the first parable, the person being loved is the wasteful son. Throughout the story, he does nothing to be deserving of love, and yet his father does love him, generously and unconditionally. Not only does he give him half of everything he owns, even at the price of impoverishing the family farm, but he also celebrates his son's return with a feast. Likewise, the theme of the second parable is also one of generous and unconditional love, offered in this case by the Samaritan to someone who is not only a complete stranger, but even worse, an enemy of his people.

Like the Samaritan and the benevolent father, a Hero for Christ must give love generously to all, whether or not they deserve it. As a Hero for Christ you must be prepared to love even your enemies. Towards that end, we must never view our adversaries as anything other than fellow human beings, deserving of love and capable of love. Our true enemy is not the specific people who stand against us, but evil itself, which is nothing but the complete absence of good. True Christian victory, therefore, lies not in defeating, humiliating or destroying your opponents, but in convincing them to join your efforts.

Pick a day, and tell each person you meet that day that you love him or her. Try your best to be loving even to those you dislike, but do not neglect those who are closest to you.

STORIES ABOUT HEROES LOVING GENEROUSLY

Óscar Romero: "Love Generously"

As the Archbishop of El Salvador, Óscar Romero saw himself in service to all the people of El Salvador, even those who opposed him most bitterly and violently. He understood that the soldiers who oppressed the people under the guise of law and the terrorists who threatened them with illegal violence were both recruited from the same masses of dispossessed poor whose cause he advocated. A destitute farm laborer, agitating for livable wages, might be a literal brother or cousin to a guardsmen dispatched to fire guns at the demonstrators. Accordingly, Romero believed it was important that even the members of the militias know they were being prayed for and embraced by the generosity of Christian love.

Nor did Romero's love stop at the boundary of the lower class. Instead, he practiced generous love at a level that was hard for many on his own side to accept, embracing even those whose greed and lust for power was at the root of El Salvador's sufferings. The wealthy rulers of the country were members of his diocese no less than the poor laborers, and his wish for them was never that they be destroyed, but always that they be redeemed.

> *I ask the faithful people who listen to me with love and devotion to pardon me for saying this, but it gives me more pleasure that my enemies listen to me. I know that the reason they listen to me is that I bear them a message of love. I don't hate them. I don't want revenge. I wish them no harm. I beg them to be converted, to come to be happy with the happiness that you faithful ones have.*
>
> Óscar Romero, *Reflections on His Life and Writings* (Dennis)

Geoffrey Griffin: "Love Generously"

Kenyan educator Geoffrey Griffin enlisted as a soldier in the British colonialist army at the beginning of the Mau Mau Rebellion in Kenya, fighting against forces composed of members of the indigenous Kikuyu ethnic group. Over time, however, he became convinced that justice was not on the side of the British, but rather on the side of the rebels fighting for Kenyan independence. Later, as a civilian working for the government, he had a chance to work with juveniles detained in the *Manyani Prison Camp*. Among the teenaged detainees were many like a young man named Geoffrey Geturo, who had simply been in the wrong place at the wrong time, and detained without reason. Many others, however, were more like another detainee named Joseph Gikubu, who, despite his youth, had sworn himself to the cause of the Mau Mau rebels. Such was the respect that Gikubu commanded among his former comrades that he had even been empowered to administer the Mau Mau Oath, a secret affirmation to fight until Kenyan independence was achieved.

For those in charge of Manyani, Mau Mau rebels such as Gikubu could only be viewed as the worst sorts of animals. Blind to the injustices of their own side, they had an image of the rebels formed entirely by reports of white settlers massacred in their sleep, and settlements burnt to the ground. Accordingly, they treated the prisoners in their care with callousness, believing that anything other than a firm hand and brutal discipline would result in disaster. It was a situation Griffin would later describe as 20,000 Kikuyus in "barbed-wire cages."

Griffin, on the other hand, had a different idea about how the detainees should be treated, especially the youth. Although he and they were still technically on opposite sides of a war, he believed the way to treat his so-called enemies was to love them generously, in accordance with Jesus' dictum "do good to those that hate you." Although he was warned that the Mau Mau rebels like Gikubu were murderers who would surely rise up, given half the chance, and slit his throat in the middle of the night, Griffin chose to be trusting rather than cautious.

Much to the surprise of his detractors, Griffin's methods quickly began to pay off. Although his new charges initially viewed him with the same burning hatred they would have felt towards any other British colonialist, they soon began to respond to his genuine care and concern. Among those whose opinion of Griffin was transformed was Joseph Gikubu. It was a fortunate meeting of the ways for both men. Not only was Gikubu instrumental later in helping Griffin found his school, he continued there as Griffin's successor, forty years after their initial encounter.

> *Mr. Gikubu was a prefect in Wamumu, so was Mr. Geturo. This is where I got to know them…because they were outstanding even among detainees…They were natural leaders and whatever I couldn't break through, they would be able to do.*
> Geoffrey Griffin, *Educating Modern Kenyans* (Otiato)

Martin Luther King, Jr.: "Love Generously"

As a result of the work by Reverend Martin Luther King, Jr. on behalf of the blacks of America, he is often seen exclusively as black America's hero, exclusively as one who worked to liberate poor, exploited and discriminated-against blacks from the prison of segregation. To see King this way, however, is to betray both his memory and his legacy. King never viewed himself as working on behalf of black America, but rather on behalf of America as a whole. What King saw that few others could perceive was that the poison of segregation was harming white and black Americans alike.

While black America was suffering physically, economically and mentally as the victims of segregation, white America was paying no less a cost morally and spiritually as the defenders of segregation. It had reached a point where the benefits of being on top of the system were not worth being associated with the crimes against humanity that segregation represented.

In addition, King's position within the black community allowed him to see a reality to which many whites were blind: that the country was on the verge of an all-out war between the races, a war which could not help but be disastrous to both sides. The injustices of segregation were too bold, they had continued too long, and the mood of the country was too volatile for peace without justice to endure.

An example of this dynamic took place one night in St. Augustine, Florida, where a group of black civil rights marchers were planning to assemble at a local church. On their way through the city they were attacked physically by a mob of hostile whites and forced to retreat.

What the mob did not realize, however, was that they were not dealing with a docile crowd of victims who were too scared or too weak to fight. Instead they were facing a group that had made a moral commitment to non-violence because of King's leadership. Even so, there were many in the crowd of marchers who had reached their breaking point. It took all of King's authority and skill to prevent his followers from striking back. Without King's intervention, there would likely have been deaths and injuries on both sides. Although the white townspeople did not realize it, King's love was generous enough to concern itself with their best interests as well as the best interests of his own followers. At a larger scale, the same was true for King in regards to the struggle of the country as a whole.

...when you come to love on this level you begin to love men not because they are likable, not because they do things that attract us, but because God loves them and here we love the person who does the evil deed while hating the deed that the person does. It is the type of love that stands at the center of the movement that we are trying to carry on in the Southland –agape.
Martin Luther King, Jr., "The Power of Nonviolence", *Strength to Love*

Gean Norman: "Love Generously"

Gean Norman was my grandmother. She had a rare ability to love even those she hardly knew, or in many cases, did not even like, and the impact of that love could be startling.

One incident in particular is imprinted in my memory. My grandparents owned a large house on the corner of a not-very-good street. Over the years that they had lived there, the neighborhood had gone steadily downhill, and my grandmother often complained about being surrounded by families whose values and standards did not match her own. One such family lived directly across the alley from my grandmother's house. They had a number of children who ran wild in the streets, seemingly without adult supervision or discipline.

One day my grandmother and I were standing outside her house when the oldest of those children came out onto his porch. He was a typically tough and surly young teenager, who always seemed to have his face in a scowl, and I had heard my grandmother speak disapprovingly of him on more than one occasion. Yet that day, perhaps, she saw something in his eyes that was invisible to me. Whatever the reason, she called him over to her side, and he, shuffling and reluctant, obeyed.

"I want you to know," she said, without introduction or preamble, "that Mr. Norman and I love you very much."

To my shock the tough young teenager dissolved into tears. Whether it had been a rough day, or whether he had not heard those words from anyone in too long a time, I do not know, but the simple declaration had an emotional impact. The lesson I learned in that moment was that everyone needs love, and that you can never offer love to a wrong person, in a wrong place or at a wrong time.

...a child must first of all feel that he is a worthwhile person who is capable of succeeding.

Gean Norman, *The Impact of Alternative Education*

CLOSING PRAYER (*inspired by* John 13:34-35)

Dear Lord, help me love others as you have first loved me. Amen. (John 13:34-35)

REFUSE YOUR ADVERSARY'S GIFTS

Again, the devil took him up onto an exceedingly high mountain,
and showed him all the kingdoms of the world,
and the glory of them;
and said to him,
"All these things will I give thee,
if you will fall down and worship me."
Then Jesus replied,
"Depart from me, Satan: for it is written,
"You shall worship the Lord your God, and serve only him."

Matthew 4:8-10

As Jesus was beginning his ministry, he traveled into the desert to spend a period of forty days in fasting, prayer and meditation. While there, he was visited by the devil, who offered him various temptations. Among these was the gift of all the cities and kingdoms of the entire world. They were all to be given into Jesus' power by the devil, if Jesus would but fall down and worship him instead of God. Jesus, however, withstood the temptations successfully.

There is an important lesson in this story for the Christian Hero: Refuse your adversary's gifts. The choices we encounter may not be as stark as that faced by Christ, but we all are tempted by dangerous gifts on a daily basis. It is important to remember that the person who gives the gift is the person who sets the agenda, and that gifts always carry with them their own set of values and beliefs. That explains both why there is power in being generous, and why one must be cautious with each gift one receives.

Identify gifts you have received, from people, from society, or even from the privileges of race and birth. Consider how those gifts may have changed or compromised your values and beliefs.

STORIES ABOUT HEROES REFUSING GIFTS

Óscar Romero:
"Refuse Your Adversary's Gifts"

Archbishop Óscar Romero of El Salvador had a deep understanding of the moral and practical dangers of accepting gifts. His refusal to accept even the gifts of his friends was a large part of what secured him his freedom from the net of bribes, political favors and complicity that imprisoned so many others within the country.

His convictions in this regard were already formed when he was still a humble priest. At the time, he had many friends among the wealthy, although he himself lived in a plain and modest room in the parish house. One week, while he was away on a journey, a group of well-to-do women from the parish decided to do something nice on Romero's behalf. So they bought a new bed, fancy curtains and other luxurious furnishing, and remade his room to match their picture of comfort and style. When Romero returned, however, he was furious rather than grateful. Before the day was over, he had given away all the new goods and reclaimed his old cot and chair.

Later, as an Archbishop, he became famous for his blanket refusal to accept any and all invitations to government events, including presidential inaugurations. He also refused all offers of police security, including the gift of a bulletproof car, knowing full well that those who offered to protect him were also those from whom he had the most to fear.

He also practiced this same principle as a representative of the El Salvadoran people. While serving in that capacity, he tried his best to refuse both military aid and so-called humanitarian aid sent from the United States to El Salvador. He knew that all funds flowing into the country from abroad would be channeled through the government, and ultimately used to support the oppression of the people.

> *I may be their friend, but they're not going to start manipulating me, no matter how much money they have!*
>
> Óscar Romero, *Memories in Mosaic* (López)

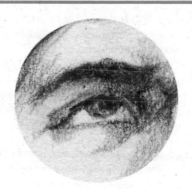

Sundar Singh:
"Refuse Your Adversary's Gifts"

Indian Christian Sádhu Sundar Singh learned at an early age the importance of being willing to refuse the gifts of others. In particular, his own moment of temptation came not long after he had converted to Christianity at age fifteen. For much of the next year, while he remained in his father's home, his relatives conspired to convince him to abandon his new-found faith and return to the beliefs of his community.

The peak of this activity came one day when a wealthy uncle invited Singh to his house alone. Taking him down beneath his mansion to a dark cellar, he opened a heavy safe and revealed the bulk of the family's wealth, including cash, jewelry and precious gems. As a final step, the uncle removed his own turban and laid it at Singh's feet, an unheard of gesture of honor and abasement from a respected elder to his young relative.

The point, of course, was to convince Singh to renounce his Christianity, and thus preserve his family's sense of honor and religious pride. Therefore, although it tempted him severely, Singh refused both his uncle's respect and his wealth. Although Singh was eventually driven out of his home, he considered the luxury that he had given up a small price to pay for his gain of Christ.

> *I began to think: "Yesterday and before that I used to live in the midst of luxury at my home; but now I am shivering here, and hungry and thirsty and without shelter, with no warm clothes and no food." I had to spend the whole night under the tree. But I remember the wonderful joy and peace in my heart, the presence of my Savior. I held my New Testament in my hand. I remember that night as my first night in heaven. I remember the wonderful joy that made me compare that time with the time when I was living in a luxurious home. In the midst of luxuries and comfort I could not find peace in my heart. The presence of the Savior changed the suffering into peace.*
> Sundar Singh, *The Message of Sádhu Sundar Singh* (Streeter)

Thomas Aquinas: "Refuse Your Adversary's Gifts"

One of the most famous and often repeated stories about Saint Thomas Aquinas concerns the year he spent in captivity in his family's castle at Roccasecca in what is now Italy. He had been kidnapped by his own brothers and brought home as a prisoner on his mother's orders, because she was dead set against him joining up with the poor, studious and devout order of Dominican monks. It was not the thought of her son becoming a monk that bothered Aquinas's mother, but the thought of his poverty. There were many monks in those days that belonged to orders with no objections to being worldly, wealthy, and materially comfortable, and she could not understand why Aquinas refused to join one of those instead.

Over the course of Aquinas's year at home, his family tried every possible form of persuasion to convince him to change his mind. At length, they hit upon a scheme they thought was sure to succeed. With an eye to Aquinas's loneliness and to the weaknesses of youth, they secured the services of a beautiful young prostitute.

Late one night, Aquinas awoke from sleep to find the prostitute dressed for seduction and standing over his bed. Instead of welcoming her into the bed, and ruining himself for the Dominicans as his family had hoped, he refused their gift by jumping up, grabbing a burning stick out of his fireplace and chasing the prostitute out of the room with it. He then slammed the door shut behind her, and scorched the sign of the cross into it with his torch. He understood that his visitor's services were not as free as they seemed, and that the price for them was not one that he wished to pay.

> *Just as God knew that man, through being tempted, would fall into sin, so too He knew that man was able, by his free will, to resist the tempter.*
> Thomas Aquinas, *Summa Theologica II-II-165*

Wilberforce: "Refuse Your Adversary's Gifts"

British abolitionist William Wilberforce learned the hard way the importance of refusing the gifts of enemies –and friends. In his childhood he had lived for several years in Wimbledon with his aunt and uncle following the death of his father. There he had adopted the quiet simplicity of their lives and the deep conviction of their faith. When he returned home to his mother's house, however, he found himself in quite a different environment.

Although his mother considered herself religious, hers was a polite, church-on-Sunday religion, rather than the passionate faith of Wilberforce's aunt and uncle. Also in contrast to them, she was a dedicated fan of the material comforts of life. As soon as Wilberforce was back in her care, she set about to take the serious little Christian her son had become and to mold him into a proper fun-loving aristocrat. At first Wilberforce resisted, trying to hold fast to the values and beliefs he had learned in Wimbledon. But he was soon overcome by the new luxuries to which he was exposed. Before long he, like his new friends, thought of nothing but pleasure and enjoyment.

Over a decade would pass before Wilberforce would finally return to his faith. When he did so it was with a deep understanding of the dangers of adversarial gifts. It was a lesson that served him well in his political career, and that allowed him to avoid the corruption that afflicted so many of his colleagues in Parliament.

My religious impressions continued for some time after my return to Hull, but no pains were spared... to stifle them... [N]o pious parent ever laboured more to impress a beloved child with sentiments of religion than [was done] to give me a taste for the world and its diversions... At first all this was very distasteful to me, but by degrees I acquired a relish for it, and so the good seed was gradually smothered, and I became as thoughtless as any amongst them.

William Wilberforce, *A Hero For Humanity* (Belmonte)

CLOSING PRAYER (*inspired by* Matthew 6:13)

Lead me not into temptation, Lord, and help me refuse all gifts except those blessed in your sight. Amen.

TURN THE OTHER CHEEK

When someone strikes you on one cheek, turn and offer him the other cheek as well, and when someone takes your cloak, offer him also your coat.

Luke 6:29

Every Christian knows that Jesus instructed us to "turn the other cheek" when attacked, but few Christians are willing to follow the instruction. Perhaps more would be willing to do so, however, if we understood the principle more fully. Not only is turning the other cheek a symbol of humility and nonresistance, it is also a powerful tactic towards victory without violence.

The secret is that most people who do bad things are not willful evildoers, but rather delusional pursuers of what they believe to be right. If you can make such persons aware of the wrongness of their attack on you, they may abandon it. Turning the other cheek, or in other words inviting a second attack from your adversary, supports this goal in three ways: First, it avoids feeding into an escalating series of attacks and counterattacks. Second, it clearly establishes that you are the victim and that your opponent is the aggressor. Third, it demonstrates your strength, both in your ability to withstand a direct attack and in your willingness to be attacked again. Ideally, this will force your opponents to reevaluate themselves and what they are doing, and perhaps choose to call off the attack. If not, however, it may still rob your opponents of their supporters, and thus of much of their power.

Identify a situation in your life where you feel attacked. What would it mean to "turn the other cheek" in that situation?

A HERO WHO TURNED THE OTHER CHEEK

Martin Luther King, Jr.: "Turn the Other Cheek"

One way of viewing Reverend Martin Luther King, Jr. is to see him as having been the general of a non-violent army. When viewed in this way, he is revealed as equal or the superior of many of the great military minds of history. He achieved victory on many fronts, and he did so with a weaker, smaller, unarmed army, and without killing or using force.

In planning his battles, King was true to the dictum of the great military genius, Sun Tzu, "To subdue the enemy without fighting is the supreme excellence." He was also following the example of the revered Indian leader Gandhi, who had shown that nonviolence could be an effective political tool. King's real inspiration, however, was using the teachings of Jesus Christ as a blueprint for effective non-violent activism.

King used this new strategy most effectively in his campaign in Birmingham. The situation he and the movement faced was this:

Black people in the South were being brutalized in a number of different ways. They were being physically attacked by the members of corrupt police forces, and by groups such as the Ku Klux Klan. They were being economically oppressed, by being forced into low-paid menial labor; and they were being spiritually attacked, by being treated as though they were less than human, by always being given the worst of everything, and by never being allowed to share in the fruits of their own labors. All of this fell in the category of what Jesus might have called the strike on the right cheek, the initial blow, the first offense.

The problem was that all these crimes were visible mainly to the victims. Those who perpetuated the indignities of segregation were often respected citizens. They saw themselves as good and upright people, and believed they were justified in their actions because they accepted the lie that black people were intended by nature to be subservient. Meanwhile, those who were physically distanced from segregation were able to ignore the situation altogether, believing it to be someone else's problem, with nothing to do with them.

It was here that King's true genius emerged. His community had already been struck. But where others might have chosen to strike back, he instead charted a course of turning the other cheek. Where a military general might have chosen to attack where the enemy was weakest, King instead elected to take his army to where the enemy was strongest, Birmingham, one of the most virulently racist strongholds of segregation in the South.

What few people ever understood was that the entire purpose of going to Birmingham was to be hit again, to be struck on the left cheek as on the right, without having done anything to deserve it other than to present it as a target. In this regard, Birmingham was ideal, largely because of the presence of city commissioner Eugene "Bull" Connor. In contrast to Laurie Pritchard, the intelligent, temperate and moderate police chief who had outmaneuvered King in Albany, Connor was a one-man representative of all of the worst aspects of segregationism. In addition to being a city commissioner, he was also a member of the Ku Klux Klan and a staunch defender of all forms of racial discrimination. He had a hot temper, a history of overreacting, and in the past had arrested people merely for meeting around the topic of civil rights. To top it all off, he had a record of political scandal, and had recently made headlines by refusing to relinquish control of the city government, even after losing a campaign to become the mayor of Birmingham.

The next few months were the most delicate and dangerous for King's plan. He had located the perfect adversary, a man who personally despised black people, and who, with his dual membership in the city government and the Ku Klux Klan, represented both the legitimate and illegitimate segregationist power structures of Birmingham. The difficulty, however, would be to maintain discipline among his own troops. It was vitally important that they play the perfect victims opposite Connor's textbook villain. Over and over King coached his followers. No matter what happened to them, no matter whether they were attacked, or spat upon, called vile names or beaten, they must not respond in kind or take any violent action whatsoever. They must remain absolutely committed to the principles of Christian non violence, even if that meant the loss of their own lives. Like soldiers marching into battle, King and his followers had to embrace risking death on a daily basis.

All that remained at that point was to present the target of the other cheek. Accordingly, King presented Connor with a variety of morally blameless provocations, including boycotts, marches and sit-ins. At first, Connor tried to respond intelligently. He staged orderly arrests, and quietly put people in jail without violence or brutality. It was at that point that King raised the ante by bringing the children of Birmingham into the movement.

Many people, even after Birmingham's success, criticized the decision to include children on the front lines, where they were at risk of their lives. What King understood, however, is that the black children of Birmingham were already being struck on the right cheek. They were already facing physical danger, the loss of opportunities, and the death of their dreams and their futures even as civilian onlookers in the struggle. To join the movement and offer the left cheek was no greater a risk than the risk of doing nothing.

Faced with the unexpected influx of hundreds of new protesters from Birmingham's own schools, Connor finally let his true colors show. There, under the glare of the cameras of the nation's media, he struck with full force at the movement's left cheek, unleashing police dogs, turning on high-powered firehoses, and allowing his policemen to club the unarmed, non-violent men, women and children of the movement.

The results were dramatic. Almost overnight, the mood of the nation shifted. It became impossible for America's white mainstream to continue to support segregation and still think of themselves as good people. By turning the other cheek, King had created an indelible image printed in stark black-and-white in newspapers from one coast to the other. On one side was the living embodiment of all the sins of segregation people would have rather ignored, the corruption of government and abuse of authority, the violence and brutality, and the lack of any human regard for those of another color, even if they were unarmed children. On the other side was a group whose moral authority and belief in the rightness of their cause was proven by their refusal to take up weapons and strike back. By the time it was all over, segregation had lost the battle for the hearts and minds of the American people. The victory belonged to King; and the strategy that produced that victory belonged to Jesus.

I had come to see early that the Christian doctrine of love operating through the Gandhian method of nonviolence was one of the most potent weapons available to the Negro in his struggle for freedom.
Martin Luther King, Jr., *The Autobiography of Martin Luther King, Jr.*

CLOSING PRAYER (*inspired by* John 16:33)

Lord, help me achieve victory without violence. Amen.

29

REFRAME CONFLICT

"Tell us therefore, what do you think?
Is it lawful to pay taxes to Caesar or not?"
But Jesus perceived their wickedness and said,
"Why do you tempt me, you hypocrites?
Show me the money for the taxes."
So they brought him a coin, and he asked them
"Whose picture and inscription are on this coin?"
When they answered "Caesar's", Jesus told them:
"Then give to Caesar what belongs to Caesar,
and to God what belongs to God."

Matthew 22:17-21

As he traveled and preached, Jesus often faced off against hostile questioners. For instance, he was once asked whether it was right to pay taxes to the Romans, the hated foreign conquerors. The question was a carefully designed trap. If Jesus answered "yes" then he would lose credibility among the Jews, but if he answered "no" then he could be denounced to the Romans and potentially arrested. Instead of giving either answer, Jesus reframed the conflict. He did so by first pointing out the picture of the Roman ruler on the coins themselves. This was a pointed reminder that his questioners were already collaborating with the Romans whether they paid their taxes or not. In other words, by even using Roman money, they had tacitly accepted Roman rule. At the same time, Jesus used the opportunity to preach the importance of giving God what God was due. Instead of catching Jesus in a trap, his adversaries found themselves listening to a sermon.

Reframing the conflict is another powerful tactic from Jesus, but available to every Christian Hero. To put it into action, take whatever your opponent throws against you, and remake it into an opportunity to spread your own message and further your own vision.

Identify a current conflict in your life. Find a way to harness the energy of the conflict for positive ends.

STORIES ABOUT HEROES REFRAMING CONFLICT

Sojourner Truth: "Reframe The Conflict"

American preacher and evangelist Sojourner Truth is best remembered for a speech that exemplified the principle of reframing the conflict. The occasion was a Women's Rights Convention in Akron, to which she had been invited by the organizer of the event, Francis Gage. Most of the hecklers who showed up uninvited to the event were as hostile to the idea of racial equality as they were to the idea of women's rights; and even many of the legitimate delegates to the convention were opposed to the inclusion of someone who was black.

On the second day of the event, a group of ministers appeared at the convention to denounce the idea of rights for women. They used quotes from the Bible to support their claims of male superiority, and managed to intimidate most of the women present into silence. It was then, as recalled years later by Gage, that Truth chose to break her silence. Adapting the popular Abolitionist motto "Am I not a Woman?" she exposed the hypocrisy of those who claimed on the one hand to be protecting and honoring the supposed weakness and fragility of women, yet who had no qualms about reserving tasks of hard and menial labor for women who were black. By setting one prejudice in opposition to another, she exposed the selfishness and mean-spiritedness inherent in both.

> *I could work as much…and eat as much as any man, when I could get it, and bear the lash as well. And ain't I a woman? I have borne children and seen them sold into slavery, and when I cried out with a mother's grief, none but Jesus heard me. And ain't I a woman?*
>
> Sojourner Truth, *"Ain't I a Woman?"*

Óscar Romero: "Reframe The Conflict"

As Archbishop Óscar Romero became increasingly vocal in his criticisms of the government, the risk grew that he would misspeak in a way his opponents could twist to use against him. The opportunity his adversaries had waited for arrived one day when he was delivering a sermon and spoke of "judges who sell themselves." Although it was common knowledge that many judges always ruled in favor of the government, presumably in exchange for payment, it would have been an extremely hard charge to prove, particularly without governmental cooperation.

Accordingly, the Salvadoran Supreme Court seized the opportunity to demand that Romero reveal the names of the judges who were "selling themselves." If Romero produced a list of names, the plan was to sue him for slander. If he failed to name names it would be a perfect opportunity to brand him as liar and a provocateur; as someone who made outrageous false accusations, but was then too cowardly to stand behind them.

Instead of falling into the trap on either side, however, Romero took his cues from how Jesus had responded when placed in a similar situation. Rather than giving his opponents an answer that they could use, he seized the opportunity to reframe the conflict. In a carefully prepared public response, he accused the members of the Supreme Court of focusing on one particular phrase only in order to distract people from the court's own complicity in the nation's wholesale violation of human rights. He went on to detail case after case in which the Supreme Court had sat idly by while the government violated its own laws and procedures. He ended by thanking the court for opening the conversation, and by challenging them to use the opportunity to seek judicial reform.

It was a masterful bit of strategy on Romero's part, but a disaster for his adversaries. They had taken what they assumed would be their opportunity to humiliate Romero in full view of the public, but had unwittingly focused the nation's attention on the very scandals they had wished to hide.

> *There is a lack of respect for one of the most sacred rights of the human person, the right to be well informed, the right to the truth.*
>
> Óscar Romero, *The Violence of Love*

CLOSING PRAYER (*inspired by* John 9:3)

Dear Lord, help me reframe each crisis I face into an opportunity to do your work. Amen.

FORGIVE YOUR ENEMIES

For if you forgive men their trespasses, your heavenly Father will also forgive you: But if you do not forgive men their trespasses, your Father will also not forgive your trespasses.
Matthew 6:14-15

When Jesus was taken to Calvary and crucified, one of the last things he said as he hung there, dying on the cross, was "Forgive them, Father, for they know not what they do." In the midst of his pain and suffering as the victim of the greatest crime in the history of the world, Jesus was still willing and able to forgive.

For the Christian Hero, forgiveness is the final step towards victory without violence. The important thing to remember is that we forgive as much or as more for our own sakes as for the sakes of those we forgive. Our forgiveness may or may not weaken the hold that evil has on our adversaries, but it will unfailingly offer us protection against that evil spreading into our own hearts.

In the normal course of events, evil grows and festers inside people until they lash out and harm others. If those others respond in kind, evil is able to spread and reproduce by growing in the hearts of the victims. If, however, the victims are forgiving, the cycle of evil is disrupted.

When we execute a murderer, we often believe we are destroying evil. The opposite, however, is true. Although we may be killing the person who housed the evil and gave it form, we are providing another home for that same evil in our own hearts and souls. We murder people on behalf of the state, and in so doing we become evil's new host.

The only true way to destroy evil is to drive it out with love. Thus we witness Jesus' own behavior when challenged to endorse the death penalty. The Pharisees brought before him a prisoner whose crime carried the mandated penalty of death under the Law of Moses, and whose guilt was not in question. Rather than participate in the execution, he acted to halt it, extended forgiveness, and counseled reform.

This is difficult even to imagine. The thought of some crimes is so horrible that it brings an involuntary reaction of anger despite every best effort. But what is Jesus asking us to do? It is neither to approve of horrible things, nor to change our minds about what we consider wrong. Rather, he is instructing us to give up on revenge, to be mindful of our own flaws, and to place everything in God's hands. What do we do in the face of remorseless, implacable evil? We deny it a place in our own hearts. In the end, who our adversaries are and what they have done to us is irrelevant. We forgive others as much for our own benefit as for theirs.

Identify those people and groups who have hurt or harmed you, your family, your community or your nation. Release your anger and extend to them your forgiveness.

STORIES ABOUT HEROES FORGIVING THEIR ENEMIES

Martin Luther King, Jr.: "Forgive Your Enemies"

Few people have understood the redemptive power of forgiveness as deeply as Martin Luther King, Jr. No matter what atrocity he faced, King's answer was always to be forgiving. Not only did this mean forgiving the injustices of segregation itself, it also meant being forgiving when friends and colleagues were shot at, beaten to death, lynched, or murdered. When his followers were attacked by dogs and firehoses, King counseled forgiveness, and he did not waver from this stance even when his own house was bombed, with his wife and infant daughter inside.

Perhaps the most severe test of King's commitment to forgiveness came on a terrible morning in September of 1963, when a bomb exploded in a church during Sunday School, killing four young girls. Even faced with the horror of this act, King held fast to his convictions, preaching a sermon of reconciliation rather than revenge over the coffins of the young victims. He understood that for a Christian, injury and even death are not defeats. It is a defeat to give in to hatred and the desire for revenge, but forgiveness is a victory over evil.

> *So in spite of the darkness of this hour we must not despair. We must not become bitter; nor must we harbor the desire to retaliate with violence. We must not lose faith in our white brothers. Somehow we must believe that the most misguided among them can learn to respect the dignity and worth of all human personality.*
>
> Martin Luther King, Jr., *The Autobiography of Martin Luther King, Jr.*

Desmond Tutu: "Forgive Your Enemies"

In 1977, Steve Biko, a respected leader of the anti-apartheid protest movement in South Africa, was arrested and beaten to death by the Port Elizabeth police. Desmond Tutu, then the Anglican bishop of Lesotho, was asked to give the eulogy at Biko's funeral. It was a tense situation, where black resentment of oppressions and crimes of the apartheid government seemed ready to spill over into open violence.

In his eulogy, however, Tutu refused to give into the temptation to preach a message of hate or revenge. Instead, he asked the mourners to realize that apartheid in South Africa had dehumanized whites as much as it had blacks. He then asked the crowd to pray for white South African leaders and policemen, not only to restore the humanity of their victims, but to regain their own humanity as well.

Tutu would later carry that same ethic of forgiveness into the post-apartheid era as the head of South Africa's Truth and Reconciliation

Commission. Under Tutu's leadership it became a unique experiment in forgiveness and healing.

The basic idea of the commission was simple: There had been too many crimes and too many deaths that had taken place under apartheid for them to simply be forgotten. At the same time, harsh punishments of the kind demanded by many within the new South African majority government would have led to more anger and bitterness. Instead, the commission offered amnesty to all those willing to confess fully to their crimes, and who could demonstrate that their acts had been politically motivated. In addition, no favoritism would be shown to one side or the other. Both members of the former apartheid-supporting government, and members of the former dissident and rebel groups that had opposed apartheid would have to submit to the same process, the same standards, and the same arbitration. At the same time, those who had been victims of violence and atrocities were encouraged to speak out about their experiences. The proceedings were then broadcast nationwide.

Although many criticized the commission for offering forgiveness rather than retribution, the commission is owed much of the credit for easing the transition between the old government and the new government, and for starting the country on a pathway of healing.

> *Jesus did not wait until those who were nailing him to the Cross had asked for forgiveness. He was ready, as they drove in the nails, to pray to his Father to forgive them... If the victim could forgive only when the culprit confessed, then the victim would be locked into the culprit's whim, locked into victimhood, whatever her own attitude or intention...*
>
> Desmond Tutu, *God Has a Dream*

Black Elk: "Forgive Your Enemies"

The Lakota religious leader Nicholas Black Elk was burdened throughout life both by his sense of himself as a key figure in the destiny of his society, and by his deep ambivalence about the responsibilities placed on his shoulders and the role he was expected to play.

The source of this confusion was a vision he had experienced as a young child. In the vision, as he later recalled it, he was brought before the spirits of nature, and entrusted with two powers: the power to heal and the power to kill. The first power was meant for the first half of his life, so that he could be a great healer and traditional doctor. The second power was meant for the second half of his life, when he was expected to become a great chief who would bring about the wholesale destruction of his people's enemies.

In his younger years, Black Elk enthusiastically accepted the first half of his supposed destiny, taking on the role of traditional healer, and taking pride and pleasure in his ability to cure sickness. He continued in this manner until a time near his fortieth birthday, which was the appointed moment for him to switch from the path of healing to the path of killing. As the date approached, however, he realized that he had no heart left for the destruction of his enemies. In his youth he had seen too much death, having been present at the massacre at Wounded Knee, in which 300 Lakota men, women and children were killed by members of the United States Army.

Instead of his memories priming him for revenge, the now middle-aged Black Elk realized that he had lost all taste for slaughter. As much as he loved his people and their traditions, his heart was calling him towards another path. As his letters reveal, he had an interest in Christianity dating back to a time during his youth when he toured with Buffalo Bill's Wild West Show. Now, on the brink of traveling the pathway of destruction, he came to a choice. Although he had once resisted the priests, and their attempts to interfere with his practice of the old ways, he now freely embraced a religion that preached forgiveness rather than revenge. Without ever losing his love and respect for Lakota tradition, he became the faithful servant of Christ that he would remain for the rest of his life.

> *So thus all along, of the white man's many customs, only his faith, the white man's beliefs about God's will, and how they act according to it, I wanted to understand.*
>
> Black Elk, *The Sixth Grandfather*

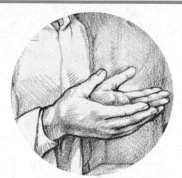

Óscar Romero: "Forgive Your Enemies"

For most people, forgiveness is difficult. They find it difficult to forgive even minor injuries, such as a harsh word or petty slight. The difficulty of forgiveness goes up again when we face larger injuries, such as the theft of property, and yet again when we face those who threaten or kill our loved ones. For most of us, forgiveness even at that level is unimaginable. Imagine, then, how much more difficult it would be to forgive your own murderer, the person who comes to take your own life. Yet this is exactly what Christ did when he prayed for his executioners, even as he hung on the cross.

This is also what Archbishop Óscar Romero did as well. He had never sought to be a martyr, and had lived sixty years in relative peace and quiet. Nor was he someone who was ready to die, or had grown tired of life. Yet it had become increasingly clear to him that he could not speak the truth as an advocate for the poor and oppressed, without becoming a target for those with the will and the ability to kill. Because of this, he was able to evaluate his life with the foreknowledge that it was destined to end violently and soon. It was a prospect that would have driven many lesser men or women mad with fear and paranoia. Romero, however, responded, like Christ, with words of forgiveness even for his approaching murderers.

> *You can tell people, if they succeed in killing me, that I forgive and bless those who do it. Hopefully, they will realize that they are wasting their time. A bishop will die, but the church of God, which is the people, will never perish.*
>
> Óscar Romero, *Reflections on His Life and Writings* (Dennis)

CLOSING PRAYER (*inspired by* Luke 23:34)

Forgive us, Father, for we know not what we do. Amen.

You are the light of the world. A city that is set on a hill cannot be hidden. Neither do men light a candle, and put it under a basket, but on a candlestick; so that it gives light unto all that are in the house. Let your light so shine before men, that they may see your good works, and glorify your Father which is in heaven.

Matthew 5:14–16

PROFILES:
22 Heroes For Christ

SAINT THOMAS AQUINAS

Thomas Aquinas was born in 1225 in the town of Roccasecca, which was then a part of the Kingdom of Naples, and is now a part of the province of Frosinone in Italy. He was the son of a nobleman, and was intended by his family to take over a lucrative post as the head of the local Benedictine monastery. Instead, Aquinas insisted on joining the rival Dominican order of monks, which existed under a vow of poverty. He there studied the works of Plato and Aristotle under the guidance of the great scientist and theologian Albertus Magnus.

At first Aquinas's classmates considered him to be dull and stupid, nicknaming him the "dumb ox" because he was quiet, shy and overweight. Despite this unpromising start he went on to have an influence on the church second only to his predecessor Augustine; and like him was declared both a Saint and a Doctor of the Roman Catholic Church. He is celebrated for his *Summa Theologica*, a comprehensive and systematic set of answers to difficult theological questions. He died on March 7, 1274, at the Cistercian Abbey of Fossanova, now a part of the province of Rome.

Notable Attributes:
Intellect, Integrity, Comprehension, Authority

Christian Principles:
Refuse Your Adversary's Gifts 179

SAINT (AURELIUS) AUGUSTINE (OF HIPPO)

Augustine was born November 13, 354 in the town of Tagaste, which is now Souk-Ahras in Algeria, and was then a part of the Roman Empire. He was a Roman citizen, and is believed to have been a member of the indigenous Berber people of North Africa. His father was a pagan, but his mother, Monica, was a devout Christian. In his youth he studied the philosophy of Plato, and later became a follower of a religion known as Manichaeanism.

He returned to Christianity at the age of thirty-two, and became Bishop of the Diocese of Hippo (now Annaba in Algeria) in his early fifties, a post he held until his death on August 28, 430. He has been criticized for having created the doctrine of the "just war," which claims that armed violence can be justified; but is primarily remembered for his autobiography, *The Confessions of Augustine*, and for his work in Christianizing the philosophies of Plato. He is considered as one of the greatest and most influential of all Christian theologians, and was declared a Saint and a Doctor of the Church by the Roman Catholic Church.

Notable Attributes:
Honesty, Humbleness, Intellect, Authority

Christian Principles:
Pray 44
Be Humble 51

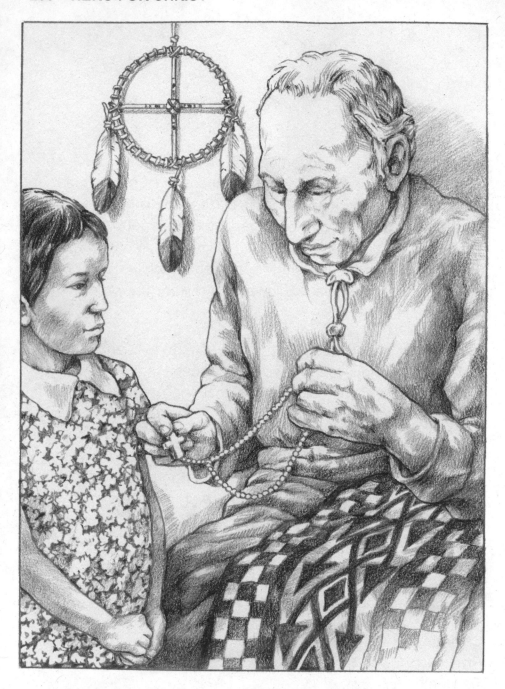

NICHOLAS BLACK ELK
(HEHAKA SAPA)

Nicholas Black Elk was born in December 1863, along the Little Powder River (now in Wyoming). He was a member of the indigenous Oglala Lakota people (formerly known as the "Sioux Indians"), and came of age at a time when the westward expansion of the United States of America was beginning to intrude on the homeland of his ancestors. As a young child, he experienced a mystical vision, and was subsequently initiated as a traditional healer for his community.

Upon reaching young adulthood he joined Buffalo Bill's Wild West Show as a way to learn more about the world and beliefs of the whites. It was here, during his travels through America and Europe, that he first encountered Christianity, which he considered to reflect some of the same truths as the religion in which he was raised. In later life he converted to Roman Catholicism (adopting the name "Nicholas") and became a catechist, or lay religious teacher. In that position he was considered personally responsible for nearly four hundred conversions to the Christian faith.

Near the end of his life, he took an interest in preserving the culture of his people, and granted interviews that became the basis for several influential books about traditional Lakota culture and religion, of which the most famous is *Black Elk Speaks*. He continues to be a controversial figure because of his attempts to reconcile his traditional Lakota beliefs with his Christian faith. He died August 19, 1950 in Manderson, South Dakota.

Notable Attributes:
Openness, Nonviolence, Mercy

Christian Principles:
Forgive Your Enemies 197

MICHELANGELO (DI LODOVICO) BUONARROTI (SIMONI)

Michelangelo was born on March 6, 1475, in the town of Caprese (now in Tuscany, Italy). Michelangelo showed both talent and interest in art at a young age, and overcame opposition from his parents to begin artistic studies at the start of his teenaged years. During his long career, he worked for Pope Julius II, Pope Leo X, Pope Clement VII, Pope Paul III, and several other influential patrons, creating masterpieces of Christian art such as *David* (1504) and the ceiling fresco of the Sistine Chapel (1512). He was criticized both during his life and after his death for his presumed homosexuality, but is better remembered for being a superlative painter and sculptor, as well as for his work as an architect and a poet. He died February 18, 1564, in Rome.

Notable Attributes:
Creativity, Artistry

Christian Principles:
Develop Your Talents 66

DOROTHY DAY

Dorothy Day was born November 8, 1897, to a Scotch-Irish family in New York City. When young, she could best be described as a "bohemian liberal", who was involved in social activism, and committed to the concept of free love. Following two extended cohabitations, a brief marriage and divorce, a clandestine abortion and a child out of wedlock, she embraced Catholicism, which led her to renounce sexual license, but intensify her commitment to social justice. Later in life she was criticized for her supposed Communist sympathies, yet she gained an international reputation due to her passionate Christian advocacy of rights for workers and the poor. She is best remembered for founding and leading the *Catholic Worker* movement and newspaper, and was declared a candidate for sainthood by the Catholic Church, following her death on November 29, 1980, in New York City.

Notable Attributes:
Courage, Integrity, Activism, Commitment

Christian Principles:
Put Faith Above "Religion" 39

GEOFFREY WILLIAM GRIFFIN

Geoffrey Griffin was born as the child of British colonialists on June 13, 1933 in Eldoret, Kenya. Upon the outbreak of the Mau Mau Rebellion, he enlisted in the colonialist army, but subsequently became a supporter of Kenyan independence. Near the end of the uprising he rescued two thousand children from a high-security detention camp, building for them a highly successful rehabilitative and educational facility. Griffin later went on to found the Kenyan National Youth Service, as well as the internationally acclaimed *Starehe Boys Centre and School*, where he served as director until his death on June 28, 2005.

He was honored as a Moran of the Order of the Burning Spear in 1970, a Moran of the Order of the Golden Heart of Kenya in 1986, and an Officer of the Order of the British Empire in 2002. He was given the Kenya National Human Rights Commission Lifetime Achievement Award in 2005. He was sometimes criticized for supporting the political *status quo* and for neglecting the education of girls; yet these failings were eclipsed by his achievement in creating a world-class educational institution serving some of the most destitute and disenfranchised children in the world. Griffin was a non-denominated Protestant.

Notable Attributes:
Inclusivity, Mentiveness, Activism, Jesus Vision, Commitment

Christian Principles:
Take Responsibility 55
Forgive Yourself and Move Forward 60
Serve the Least 78
Be Inclusive 83
Honor Service 102
Mentor Others 108
Invest in People 122
Be Committed 141
Love Generously 169

MAHALIA (MAHALA) JACKSON

Mahalia Jackson was born out-of-wedlock to a poor black family in New Orleans on October 26, 1912. After being orphaned as a child, she was raised by her aunt until the age of fifteen, when she moved to Chicago. There she joined a gospel band at a Baptist church, and later embarked on a solo career after teaming up with the talented gospel composer Thomas A. Dorsey. Her big break in the music business came when her recordings were popularized by radio host Studs Terkel. By the time of her death, she had an international reputation as the greatest living gospel singer. She was often criticized for her love of money; yet she was also known for acts of great generosity towards friends, family and strangers. Her honors included the Silver Dove Award, the French Academy of Music Award, the Grammy Lifetime Achievement Award, and induction into the Rock and Roll Hall of Fame. She died on January 27, 1972 in Evergreen Park, Illinois.

Notable Attributes:
Artistry, Integrity

Christian Principles:
Put God First 18
Find Your Own Path 24
Live Your Faith 72
Maximize Your Resources 118

REVEREND TOYOHIKO KAGAWA
(KAGAWA TOYOHIKO)

Kagawa was born July 10, 1888, in Kobe, Japan, the son of a businessman and his geisha concubine. He was orphaned while young and taken in by his father's legitimate wife. Neglected at home, he was mentored by missionaries, and converted to Christianity, eventually becoming a minister in the Japanese Presbyterian church. Upon reaching adulthood, he became a strong advocate of Christian pacifism, a stance which made him a frequent target of criticism at home in Japan.

He was also an advocate of the social gospel, eventually becoming a founder of Japan's first labor union, as well as an organizer of a number of cooperative farming and lending organizations. He was a part of the transitional government that offered surrender to the United States at the end of World War II. He received the Order of the Sacred Treasure of Japan and was nominated for the 1955 Nobel Peace Prize. He died April 23, 1960 in Tokyo.

Notable Attributes:
Thrift, Activism, Generosity, Nonviolence, Prodigal Love, Commitment, Integrity

Christian Principles:
Pray 46   Serve the Least 79
Live Your Faith 71   Value Each Individual 91
Be Open Minded 153
Stand Up for What You Believe 31
Put Faith Above "Religion" 40
Maximize Your Resources 119
Forgive the Sins and Debts of Others 97

REVEREND DOCTOR
MARTIN LUTHER (MICHAEL) KING, JR.

Martin Luther King, Jr. was born on January 15, 1929 in Atlanta, Georgia. His father was the prominent pastor of a local black Baptist church, and King followed in his father's footsteps as soon as he reached adulthood. As a social activist, King was instrumental in finding a moral and non-violent way to fight and overcome legally sanctioned racism and injustice in the American South of the 1950's and 1960's.

Although criticized for his extramarital affairs, King received a multitude of honors including the 1964 Nobel Peace Prize, the 1965 American Liberties Medallion, the 1966 Margaret Sanger Award, the 1971 Grammy Award for Best Spoken Word Recording for "Why I Oppose the War in Vietnam", and the 1977 US Presidential Medal of Freedom. He was assassinated on April 4, 1968 in Memphis, Tennessee.

Notable Attributes:
Courage, Activism, Nonviolence, Oratory, Mercy, Inclusivity, Vision, Prodigal Love

Christian Principles:

Put God First 16	Be Bold 129
Serve the Least 77	Be Inclusive 84
Attend to the Details 135	Be Persistent 146
Find Your Own Path 26	Be Ready 159
Love Generously 171	Honor Service 101
Develop Your Talents 65	
Forgive Your Enemies 194	
Turn the Other Cheek 183	
Forgive Yourself and Move Forward 59	
Forgive the Sins and Debts of Others 96	
Maximize Your Resources 115	
Stand Up for What You Believe 29	

CLIVE ("JACK") STAPLES LEWIS

C. S. Lewis was born November 29, 1898 in Belfast, Northern Ireland. He was born into a religious family, but had lost his faith by the age of thirteen, becoming instead a committed atheist. After reaching adulthood, however, his opinions once again began to shift, to the point where he decided that belief in God was more reasonable and rational than disbelief in God and that Christianity was demonstrably the best of all religions.

He joined the Anglican Church, and subsequently became famous for a series of books aimed at guiding skeptics towards a robust and confident embrace of Christianity. Although sometimes criticized for peculiarities in his views and weaknesses in his arguments, his writings remain popular and influential because of their readability and intellectual depth. In addition to his theological works, he is also remembered for his Christian-themed fiction, most notably his classic series of children's fantasy, *The Chronicles of Narnia*. He died on November 22, 1963 in Oxford, England.

Notable Attributes:
Intellect, Creativity, Openness

Christian Principles:
Develop Your Talents 63

SAINT THÉRÈSE (THERESA) DE LISIEUX (MARIE-FRANÇOISE-THÉRÈSE MARTIN)

Thérèse was born on January 2, 1873 in Alençon, France, the youngest daughter of a French watchmaker. She joined the Carmelite nuns at the age of fifteen. At the age of twenty-two she contracted tuberculosis. She died two years later, on September 30, 1897, in Lisieux, France, but not before writing an influential book detailing what came to be known as the "Little Way" of mindful obedience to God in each small detail of life. Although her writing is sometimes criticized as overly sentimental, she was subsequently sainted by the Catholic Church and is one of only three women to be honored as a Doctor of the Church.

Notable Attributes:
Humbleness, Patience, Comprehension, Faith, Authority

Christian Principles:
Be Humble 52
Attend to the Details 132

MARTIN LUTHER

Martin Luther was born on November 10, 1483 in Eisleben, Saxony (which was then part of the Holy Roman Empire, and is now in Germany). He originally studied to become a lawyer, but entered a monastery after being narrowly saved from a strike of lightning during a thunderstorm. After intense study, he received a doctorate in theology and took up a post in the parish of Wittenberg.

In 1517, he published his famous "Ninety-Five Theses" criticizing corruption within Catholicism (which, according to legend, he nailed to the door of the church). These and subsequent writings made Luther the central figure in the nascent Reformation movement, and led first to the banning of his writings, and eventually to his excommunication. In modern times he has come under criticism for writings attacking Jews and peasants; yet he continues to be honored as the father of tho Protestant Reformation, and a major influence on the so-called Counter-Reformation within the Catholic Church. He died February 18, 1546 in Eisleben.

Notable Attributes:
Integrity, Vision, Intellect, Authority, Courage

Christian Principles:
Put Faith Above "Religion" 37
Be Humble 50

MARY AND MARTHA

Mary and Martha were sisters from a town called Bethany. They were two of Jesus' most important female disciples, and they, along with their brother Lazarus, are described as being particularly beloved by Jesus. They are mentioned several times in the gospels, including in the Gospel of Luke, where Martha spends her time doing household chores while Mary sits at Jesus' feet, in the Gospel of John, where Jesus raises their brother Lazarus from the dead, and again in the Gospel of John where Mary anoints Jesus with ointment and wipes his feet with her hair.

On two of these occasions, Mary is criticized by others, first Martha, who accuses her of being too lazy to help with the chores, and second Judas Iscariot, who claims that her use of costly ointment is wasteful. In both cases, however, Mary's choices are confirmed by Jesus as right and proper expressions of devotion.

Notable Attributes: Faith, Commitment

Christian Principles:
Put God First 13
Be Committed 138

DOCTOR
GEAN ALICE (GILMORE) NORMAN

Gean Norman was born on January 28, 1914 in Marlinton, West Virginia, and grew up as a Baptist. She graduated college in the 1930's, at a time when that was still a rare distinction for a black woman in America, and later went on to complete a doctorate. A lifelong educator and child-advocate, she was an influential figure in local education in Columbus, Ohio. She there played an important role in racial desegregation, the formation of the "alternative" schools program and the placement of counselors in elementary schools. She died August 6, 2005 in Columbus.

Notable Attributes:
Jesus Vision, Mentiveness, Prodigal Love

Christian Principles:
Love Generously 173

SAINT AND APOSTLE
SIMON "PETER" ("CEPHUS")

Peter was an uneducated fisherman who became one of Jesus' most important and influential disciples. Jesus described him as the "Rock," the foundation of the church, and the keeper of the keys of heaven. He was sometimes criticized because of his denial of Christ and his disputes with the Apostle Paul, yet he was the first to receive the teaching that opened the church to non-Jews, and was the founder of many of the first Christian churches. According to the Catholic tradition, Peter was the first Pope. He was later crucified, and according to legend, requested to be crucified head-down because he did not feel worthy of the same death as Jesus.

Notable Attributes: Faith, Humbleness, Honesty, Commitment, Courage, Activism, Inclusivity, Authority, Menliveness

Christian Principles:
Forgive Yourself & Move Forward 57
Mentor Others 104
Invest In People 121
Be Bold 125
Be Open Minded 149
Be Ready 157

ARCHBISHOP ÓSCAR ARNULFO ROMERO Y GALDÁMEZ

Óscar Romero was born August 15, 1917, in Ciudad Barrios, San Miguel, El Salvador. He was originally considered a conservative and apolitical religious leader. Shortly after he was confirmed as the Catholic Archbishop of San Salvador, his friend Father Rutilio Grande was assassinated, presumably on orders from the Salvadoran government. The subsequent refusal of the government to investigate the death awakened Romero to the reality of brutality and corruption among members of the military oligarchy ruling the country. For the next three years he was an outspoken advocate of freedom and justice, until his own assassination, March 24, 1980 in San Salvador, El Salvador. Although many criticized his politicized religious beliefs, there were just as many who celebrated his advocacy of "liberation theology." He was nominated for the Nobel Peace Prize in 1979.

Notable Attributes:
Courage, Activism, Integrity, Commitment, Oratory

Christian Principles:
Stand Up for What You Believe 32
Put Faith Above "Religion" 41
Love Generously 168
Refuse Your Adversary's Gifts 176
Reframe the Conflict 190
Forgive Your Enemies 198

SÁDHU SUNDAR SINGH

Sundar Singh was born September 3, 1889, to wealthy Sikh parents in Rampur, Patiala, North India. He was violently opposed to Christianity as a young teenager. At age fifteen he was on the verge of suicide when he experienced a powerful vision of the living Christ. He immediately converted to Christianity, and was subsequently thrown out of his home. He studied for some time at an Anglican seminary, but decided he could best preach Christianity to other Indians if he presented himself in a more familiar form. Accordingly, he took on the robes of a *sádhu* or holy man, and spent the rest of his life wandering from place to place, with neither money nor a permanent home, preaching the gospel wherever he went. Although baptized and trained as an Anglican, he refused to align himself with any one denomination over another. During his life he was sometimes criticized for what was seen as his excessive mysticism, yet he gained a worldwide reputation for holiness and devotion to Christ. He disappeared on a mission trip to the Himalayas of Tibet in 1929.

Notable Attributes:
Humbleness, Thrift, Faith, Focus, Integrity, Prodigal Love, Courage

Christian Principles:

Put God First 19	Be Persistent 144
Find Your Own Path 22	Do Not Resist Evil Persons 164
Pray 45	Refuse Your Adversary's Gifts 177
Be Humble 49	
Value Each Individual 92	
Maximize Your Resources 117	

MOTHER TERESA
("AGNES" GONXHA BOJAXHIU)

Mother Teresa was born August 26, 1910, in the town of Skopje (which is now in Macedonia). She was Albanian by ethnicity. Mother Teresa was the founder of the Missionaries of Charity, an international group of nuns in service to the poorest of the poor. This group, together with numerous auxiliary organizations also founded or inspired by Mother Teresa, is currently active in Christian service in over 130 different countries around the world.

Although she has recently been criticized for her friendships with dictators and her willingness to accept the political *status quo,* she is globally revered for her work with the poor. Her numerous honors include the 1971 Pope John XXIII Peace Prize, the 1971 Kennedy Prize, the 1972 Nehru Prize, the 1975 Albert Schweitzer International Prize, the 1979 Balzan Prize for Humanity, Peace and Brotherhood Among Peoples, the 1979 Nobel Peace Prize, and the 1980 Bharat Ratna. She was also awarded the British Order of Merit in 1983, the U.S. Presidential Medal of Freedom, and the U.S. Congressional Gold Medal in 1994. She died September 5, 1997 in Kolkata (Calcutta), India.

Notable Attributes:
Humbleness, Thrift, Activism, Generosity, Vision, Jesus Vision, Focus, Prodigal Love, Persistence

Christian Principles:

Put God First 15

Find Your Own Path 25

Serve the Least 76

Be Inclusive 86

Invest in People 123

Forgive the Sins of Others 95

Maximize Your Resources 116

Do Not Resist Evil Persons 162

Be Bold 128

Attend to the Details 136

Be Open Minded 152

Value Each Individual 89

Be Persistent 147

Sojourner Truth (Isabelle Baumfree Van Wagenen)

Sojourner Truth was born around 1797, in Ulster County, New York. She was born a slave, but reached adulthood as New York began a process of gradual emancipation. After a religious experience, she became a committed (but non-denominated) Christian, and later became an itinerant preacher, changing her name to "Sojourner Truth" to commemorate her new calling.

She endured controversy early in life due to her association with an apocalyptic Christian cult, the "Kingdom of Matthias," but later became much celebrated as a public speaker. Throughout her long life, she was an active and influential opponent of slavery and an advocate of civil rights for all people. She died November 26, 1883 in Battle Creek, Michigan.

Notable Attributes:
Courage, Activism, Oratory

Christian Principles:
Reframe the Conflict 189

ARCHBISHOP DESMOND MPILO TUTU

Desmond Tutu was born October 7, 1931, in Klerksdorp, South Africa.   He was one of the first black South Africans to rise to a position of authority within the Anglican Church, eventually becoming the first black Archbishop of the region. Throughout his long career with the church, he was known both for his brave and bold statements of opposition to apartheid and for his unwavering support for non-violent solutions to his country's problems.

Although often criticized for his social activism, he is widely respected for his consistent Christian witness against injustice. Following his retirement, he became a key figure in the peaceful transition to a post-apartheid government through his work as the head of the Truth and Reconciliation Committee. He has received many honors, including the Albert Schweitzer Prize for Humanitarianism, the 1986 Magubela Prize for Liberty, and the 2005 Gandhi Peace Prize.

Notable Attributes:
Courage, Nonviolence, Activism, Mercy, Prodigal Love

Christian Principles:
Forgive Your Enemies 195

WILLIAM WILBERFORCE

William Wilberforce was born on August 24, 1759 in Kingston-on-Hull, England, into the family of a wealthy merchant. During a period spent with his aunt and uncle as a young child, he became a convert to their evangelical Methodism. As this was considered a disreputable religion at the time, his mother discouraged his religious views and encouraged him to lose himself in more worldly pleasures and ambitions.

Upon reaching adulthood he entered politics, rediscovered his faith, and devoted the rest of his life to social issues, most notably the abolition of slavery in Britain. During his life, he was sometimes criticized for his support of censorship and other government infringements of civil liberties; yet he remains celebrated not only for his defeat of slavery, but also for his wide-ranging social reforms. He died on July 29, 1833, in London.

Notable Attributes:
Nonviolence, Persistence, Commitment, Integrity, Patience

Christian Principles:
Stand Up for What You Believe 34
Live Your Faith 70
Mentor Others 107
Be Bold 126
Attend to the Details 133
Be Committed 139
Be Persistent 145
Be Open Minded 151
Be Ready 158
Refuse Your Adversary's Gifts 180

HEROIC ATTRIBUTES

PERSONAL VIRTUES

Commitment: The willingness to make sacrifices for your goals.

Courage: The willingness to risk harm or death for your beliefs.

Faith: The willingness to trust God absolutely.

Honesty: The willingness to be open about personal failings.

Humbleness: The refusal to be prideful about personal accomplishments and traits.

Integrity: The ability to hold onto your beliefs, values and personal identity in the face of opposition.

Patience: The ability to wait.

Persistence: The ability to keep trying despite setbacks.

Thrift: The commitment to use all resources fully.

SOCIAL VIRTUES

Activism: The ability to translate beliefs into actions.

Empathy: The ability to understand difficult things with the heart.

Generosity: The willingness to share all resources freely.

Inclusivity: The willingness and ability to include people of all descriptions in your community.

Jesus Vision: The ability to see people as their best possible selves.

Mentiveness: The ability to teach and nurture others.

Mercy: The willingness to forgive.

Focus: The ability to pursue your goals without being distracted by the provocations of others.

Nonviolence: The commitment to never respond to any provocation with violence.

Openness: The willingness to consider all possibilities.

Prodigal Love: The ability to love freely and unconditionally.

TALENTS

Artistry: The ability to create beauty.

Authority: The ability to write or rule decisively on a topic.

Vision: The ability to see the big picture and to plan for the long term.

Comprehension: The ability to grasp and take care of the entirety of the small details.

Creativity: The ability to see things differently than others.

Intellect: The ability to understand complex things with the mind.

Oratory: The ability to move people with your words.

BIBLIOGRAPHY

Aquinas, Thomas, translated by the Fathers of the English Dominican Province, *The Summa Theologica of St. Thomas Aquinas,* Second and Revised Edition, 1920

Belmonte, Kevin, *William Wilberforce: A Hero for Humanity*, Zondervan, Grand Rapids, 2007.

Bernard, Jacqueline, *Journey Toward Freedom: The Story of Sojourner Truth*, W.W.Norton & Company, Inc., New York, 1967.

Black Elk, Nicholas, with John G. Neihardt, edited by Raymond J, DeMaillie, *The Sixth Grandfather: Black Elk's Teachings, Given to John G. Neihardt*, University of Nebraska Press, Lincoln, 1984.

Bokenkotter, Thomas, *Church and Revolution: Catholics in the Struggle for Democracy and Social Justice*, Doubleday, New York, 1998.

Buonarraoti, Michelangelo, translated by John Frederick Nims, *The Complete Poems of Michelangelo*, University of Chicago Press, Chicago, 1998

Chesterton, Gilbert K., *What's Wrong With the World,* Dodd, Mead and Company, New York, 1910.

The City, "Mother Teresa Plans AIDS Home", *New York Times*, October 26, 1985.

The City, "Prisons to Release Victims of AIDS", *New York Times*, January 7, 1986.

Day, Dorothy, *The Long Loneliness*, Harper & Row, New York, 1952.

Dennis, Marie, Renny Golden and Scott Wright, *Oscar Romero: Reflections on his Life and Writings*, Orbis Books, Maryknoll, 2000.

Erdozaín, Plácido, translated by John McFadden and Ruth Warner, *Archbishop Romero: Martyr of Salvador,* Orbis Books, Maryknoll, 1980.

Farmer, David Hugh, *The Oxford Dictionary of Saints*, Oxford University Press, Oxford, 1978.

Fey, Harold E. and Margaret Frakes, *The Christian Century Reader: Representative Articles, Editorials, and Poems Selected From More Than Fifty Years of The Christian Century,* Books for Libraries Press, Freeport, 1972.

Forest, Jim, *Love Is the Measure: A Biography of Dorothy Day*, Orbis Books, Maryknoll, 1994.

Frady, Marshall, *Martin Luther King, Jr.*, Viking, New York, 2002.

Furneaux, Robin, *William Wilberforce*, Hamish Hamilton, London, 1974.

Gish, Steven D., *Desmond Tutu: A Biography*, Greenwood Press, London, 2004.

Griffin, Geoffrey, *School Mastery: Straight Talk about Boarding School Management in Kenya*. Lectern Publications Ltd., Nairobi, 1994.

Green, Roger Lancelyn and Walter Hooper, *C.S.Lewis: A Biography*, Harcourt Brace Jovanovich, New York, 1974.

Harrison, Kathryn, *Saint Thérèse of Lisieux*, Lipper/Viking, New York, 2003.

Hongo, K. O. A., & Mugambi, J. N. K. (2000). *Starehe Boys' Centre: School and Institute. The First Forty Years 1959-1999*. Nairobi: Acton Publishers.

Howes, John, "Kagawa Toyohiko", *Encyclopedia of Religion. Vol. 8. 2nd ed.* Macmillan Reference, Detroit, 2005.

Kagawa, Toyohiko, *Brotherhood Economics*, Harper & Brothers, New York, 1936.

Kagawa, Toyohiko, translated by William Axling, *Christ and Japan*, Friendship Press, New York, 1934.

Kagawa, Toyohiko, translated by Helen F. Topping and Marion R. Draper, *Meditations on the Cross*, Willett, Clark & Company, Chicago, 1935.

Kirk, John A. *Martin Luther King, Jr.: Profiles In Power*, Pearson Education Limited, Harlow, 2005.

King, Martin Luther, Jr., edited by Clayborne Carson, *The Autobiography of Martin Luther King, Jr.,* Warner Books, Inc., New York, 1998.

King, Martin Luther, Jr., *Where Do We Go From Here: Chaos or Community?,* Harper & Row, New York, 1967.

King, Martin Luther, Jr., edited by James Melvin Washington. *I Have A Dream: Writings and Speeches that Changed the World*, HarperSanFrancisco, San Francisco, 1986.

King, Martin Luther, Jr. *Strength to Love*, Fortress Press, Philadelphia, 1963.

King, Martin Luther, Jr., *Stride Toward Freedom: The Montgomery Story*, Harper & Row, New York, 1958.

Kramer, Barbara, *Mahalia Jackson: The Voice of Gospel and Civil Rights*, Enslow Publishers, Berkeley Heights, 2003.

López Vigil, Maria, translated by Kathy Ogle, *Oscar Romero: Memories in Mosaic*, EPICA, Washington, 2000.

Luther, Martin, *Luther's Works: Volume 54*, edited and translated by Theodore G. Tappert, *Volume 31*, edited and translated by Harold J. Grimm, Fortress Press, Philadelphia, 1967.

Martin, Roger, *Anthem of Bugles: The Story of Starehe Boys' Centre and School*, Heinemann Educational Books, Nairobi, 1978

McKim, Donald, K., *The Cambridge Companion to Martin Luther*, Cambridge University Press, Cambridge, 2003.

Murray, Linda, *Michelangelo*, Thames and Hudson, London, 1992.

Norman, Gean Gilmore, *Impact of Alternative Education on Achievement, Self-Concept and Perceived Behavior of Elementary School Pupils (dissertation)*, The Ohio State University, 1981.

Omolo, O. "The power of purpose", *Kenya Times*, July 10, 2005.

Otiato, Peter C., *Educating Modern Kenyans: Dr. Geoffrey William Griffin and Starehe Boys Centre and School* (dissertation manuscript), March, 2007.

Parker, Mrs. Arthur, *Sadhu Sundar Singh: Called of God*, Fleming H. Revell Company, London, 1920.

Pine-Coffin, R.S. , *Saint Augustine: Confessions*, Dorset Press, New York, 1961.

Raphael, Maryanne, *Mother Teresa, Called to Love*, Writer's World (International Press) Waverly, Ohio, 2000.

Romero, Oscar, edited and translated by James R. Brockman, *The Violence of Love,* Plough Publishing House, Farmington, 1998.

Schulke, Flip and Penelope Orter McPhee, "King Remembered," W.W. Norton & Company, Inc, New York, 1986.

Schwerin, Jules, *Got To Tell It: Mahalia Jackson, Queen of Gospel*, Oxford University Press, New York, 1992.

Simon, Charlie May, *A Seed Shall Serve: The Story of Toyohiko Kagawa, Spiritual Leader of Modern Japan*, E.P. Dutton& Company, Inc., New York, 1958.

Singh, Sundar, *The Search After Reality*, Christian Literature Society, 1968.

Streeter, B. H. and A.J. Appasamy, *The Message of Sadhu Sundar Singh: A Study of Mysticism on Practical Religion*, Macmillan Company, New York, 1922.

Tanghe, Omer, *For the Least of My Brothers: The Spirituality of Mother Teresa & Catherine Doherty*, Alba, New York, 1989.

Mother Teresa, edited by Brother Angelo Devananda, *Total Surrender,* Servant Publications, Ann Arbor, 1985.

Thérèse, de Lisieux, Saint, translated by Taylor, Thomas N., *Soeur Thérèse of Lisieux*, Burns, Oates & Washbourne, London, 1912.

Tutu, Desmond, *with Douglas Abrams*, *God Has A Dream*, Doubleday, New York, 2004.

Tutu, Naomi, *The Words of Desmond Tutu,* Newmarket Press, New York, 1989.

Varsari, Giorgio, *Lives of the Artists*, Penguin Books, London, 1965.

Yancey, Philip, *Soul Survivor,* Doubleday, New York, 2001.

Whitman, Alden, "Mahalia Jackson, Gospel Singer, And a Civil Rights Symbol, Dies", *New York Times,* January 28, 1972.

Wordsworth, William, *The Complete Poetical Works,* Macmillan and Co., London, 1888.

INDEX

ACKNOWLEDGEMENTS

To *Yeshua Messiah* (Jesus Christ), my Lord and Savior, and the inspiration for this book. To my beautiful wife April, and to my parents John and Marialyce for their constant love and support during the long process of writing and revising. To those whose work in youth ministry first influenced me to adopt a life of faith: Ginny Christopherson, Pauline Swinehart, Keith Smeltzer, Mary Dee Wiseman, Craig Vander Veen and Chris Clough. To all the pastors who have shaped and nurtured that faith: Stacy Evans, Robert Alexander, David Meredith, Pauline Allen, Martin McLee, John Edgar and Donita Harris. To all the other members of my church families at the Broad Street United Methodist Church in Columbus, the 1992 Tennessee Outreach Project (Mountain T.O.P.), the Union United Methodist Church in Boston, the 1993-1997 Swarthmore Protestant Community (*Caritas*), and the United Methodist Church for All People (*http://www.4allpeople.org/index.html*). To those whose feedback and advice helped shaped this book: Jennifer Sunami, Jesse Zalatan, Craig Blazakis, Tommy Ferguson, Andrea Donaldson, Choi and Laura Thomas, Gary, Carol and David Wright, Brad Mitchell, Yale Landsberg, the Men's Study Group of Broad Street UMC, the Friday Study Group of the UMC for All People and many more. To Peter Otiato Ojiambo for sharing his original research on Geoffrey Griffin (now published under the title "Teaching Beyond Teaching") and for his support of this project. To Maryanne Raphael (*http://www.authorsden.com/maryanneraphael*), for her advance praise of this work, and for her book *Mother Teresa, Called to Love* which was a key resource in my research; to Luis Cortés, Jr. of Esperanza USA (*http://www.esperanza.us*) and to Jim Ball of the Evangelical Environmental Network (*http://www.creationcare.org*) for their advance praise of this book and support of its publication. To Orbis Books, Gospel Light, and the Estate of Dr. Martin Luther King Jr. for permissions to reprint quotations. To the many Christian authors from whom I drew inspiration in creating this book, including Søren Kierkegaard, Karen Armstrong, Charles Sheldon, Rick Warren, Rudy Rasmus, Philip Yancey, Jim Wallis, Cecil Williams, Anne Lamott and many others. To my grandparents, Gean and Henry Norman, Soichi and Sueko Sunami, and to the rest of my family: the Sunamis, the Kopelsons, the Normans and the entire Williams-Gilmore clan. To all other friends and family members whom I have relied upon throughout the years. To Archbishop Desmond Tutu for taking time out of his busy schedule to read advance excerpts from the book; and last but certainly not least, to the rest of the Christian heroes profiled in this book, whose brave and faithful acts were a constant challenge and inspiration to me throughout my writing.

Hero For Christ - TESTIMONIAL

If you would like to offer words of support for "Hero For Christ" please feel free to copy or remove this form from this book and send it to the address below.

(ORDERING INFORMATION AVAILABLE ON REVERSE)

Testimonials
Happenstance Press / Kitoba Books
413 Fairwood Ave
Columbus, OH 43205
tel:(614)253-0453
fax:(614)253-0257

Name: _____

Title or Self Description   _____
(i.e. "Pastor"):

_____

Address: _____

City: _____   State: _____   Zip: _____

Contact Info: _____

Testimonial:

I agree that my statement as written above may be used in any manner by Happenstance Press in support of the book Hero For Christ.

Signed: _____ *Date:* _____

Hero For Christ - ORDER FORM

Please check *http://heroforchrist.com* for up-to-date availability and ordering information.

SPECIAL DISCOUNTS AVAILABLE FOR LARGE ORDERS AND FOR ORDERS BY **CHURCHES** OR OTHER **NON-PROFIT ORGANIZATIONS**

Orders
Happenstance Press / Kitoba Books
413 Fairwood Ave
Columbus, OH 43205
tel:(614)253-0453
fax:(614)253-0257

Price Per Book $16.95 + $1.15 Sales Tax = $18.10
Shipping $4.00 for the first book
$2.00 for each additional book

Please pay in US currency by **money order only** if ordering through the mail.

Name: _____

Address: _____

City: _____ State: _____ Zip: _____

Phone: _____

Email: _____

Total Books Ordered: _____

Total Amount Enclosed: $ _____ . ____